200 barbecue

hamlyn | all colour cookbook

200 barbecue recipes

Louise Pickford

An Hachette UK company
www.hachette.co.uk

First published in Great Britain in 2009 by Hamlyn,
a division of Octopus Publishing Group Ltd
2–4 Heron Quays, London E14 4JP
www.octopusbooks.co.uk

ISBN: 978-0-600-61860-7

A CIP catalogue record for this book is available
from the British Library

Printed and bound in China

1 2 3 4 5 6 7 8 9 10

Both metric and imperial measurements have been given
in all recipes. Use one set of measurements only, and not
a mixture of both.

Standard level spoon measurements are used in all recipes.
1 tablespoon = one 15 ml spoon
1 teaspoon = one 5 ml spoon

All cooking times on the barbecue are approximate,
as they may be affected by such factors as altitude,
wind, outside temperature and desired doneness.

Ovens should be preheated to the specified temperature
– if using a fan-assisted oven, follow the manufacturer's
instructions for adjusting the time and the temperature.

Fresh herbs should be used unless otherwise stated.

Medium eggs should be used unless otherwise stated.

The Department of Health advises that eggs should not be
consumed raw. This book contains some dishes made with
raw or lightly cooked eggs. It is prudent for vulnerable
people such as pregnant and nursing mothers, invalids, the
elderly, babies and young children to avoid uncooked or
lightly cooked dishes made with eggs. Once prepared, these
dishes should be kept refrigerated and used promptly.

contents

introduction

introduction

The great thing about barbecues is they represent summer, and cooking and eating outdoors is about as good as it gets. Light evenings, warm weather and the aroma of meat caramelizing over hot coals or a gas barbecue is pure bliss and is perhaps why this age-old method of cooking has evolved from the simple need to eat to the pleasurable social occasion it is today.

Although sources differ as to its origin, it is more or less recognized that the word 'barbecue' comes from the Spanish word *barbacoa*, which literally means a wooden framework used to smoke meat or fish, or as a framework to sleep in!

By the eighteenth century, however, it was used to describe a means of roasting food over heat around which an entertainment event took place, and it was the Taino peoples of the Caribbean and Florida who then used the term 'Taino Barbecu' or 'sacred pit of fire'.

From here, this method of cooking travelled throughout the American Deep South during the days of slavery, where barbecues became an important part of the social gatherings of the day. It is likely that during this period pork would have been the most common food cooked at a barbecue, as pigs were cheap. In fact, today in the US pork is still the most commonly barbecued meat.

Americans have adopted barbecuing as an important part of their culture, from barbecued ribs and steaks to the many types of fast-food joints selling burgers and the like.

Barbecuing is an excuse to get outdoors, where food seems to taste better. The food tends to be more casual and the occasion more relaxed. I think that for many of us, barbecuing has become one of our preferred methods of cooking as well as an enjoyable way of entertaining. It is a great way to cook, not only for the flavour of the food but because it's done outdoors, where we are more relaxed, informal and often happier.

types of barbecue

There are two main types of barbecue in common use and these are charcoal (or wood) and gas. They all have their advantages and disadvantages, but what they all do is cook food on a rack or grill set above the heat source. Generally, we use a barbecue to cook food over a high heat for a short amount of time, but they can also be used to great effect to slow-cook meat, often with the addition of wood chips to give a wonderful smoky flavour. I have included several recipes where you will require a barbecue with a lid, so the method becomes similar to using a conventional oven. However, the majority of the recipes can be cooked in the normal way on either a gas or charcoal barbecue.

Which is best: charcoal or gas? For flavour, I would always choose a charcoal barbecue (wood can also be used), but for convenience I have to say gas wins hands down, especially if you are only cooking for two.

charcoal barbecues

These are designed to burn coal or wood. Food cooked over coals or wood has that distinctive smoky, caramelized flavour we love so much – the outside of the food is sticky and chargrilled while the inside remains moist and succulent. However, they are messy, take longer to preheat and need constant attention.

For price and convenience, disposable charcoal barbecue sets available from many supermarkets are ideal for dinner for two.

There are also several small portable barbecues available from hardware stores and specialist suppliers, which are ideal for picnics. They are usually vented to help increase or decrease the heat, or have a rung system above the coals so the grill rack can be raised or lowered as necessary.

The 'table' barbecue is basically a box on legs – the coals sit on a grate in the box with the grill rack for cooking on top of that. The

9

rack can be raised higher or lower depending on the heat required. These often have lids.

The kettle barbecue is particularly versatile, as its shape allows the coals to sit on a grate in the drum, protected from draughts. The cooking rack sits on top and then a large dome-shaped lid can be used as a cover, transforming it into an oven. There is also a vent system that makes it easier to control the temperature.

fuels
Charcoal briquettes are the most common fuel and these are readily available from many supermarkets and hardware stores. Always read packet labels, as some briquettes can contain chemicals. Hardwood lump charcoal, which contains no additives, burns easily, heats up quickly and lasts well, is harder to find, but try specialist barbecue suppliers. If burning wood, only use hardwoods such as hickory, mesquite or oak. Apple and olive wood are also good. Wood chips are smaller chips of the same wood but these are used to create extra smoke for flavour.

lighting charcoal
Arrange a good layer of charcoal about 10 cm (4 inches) deep in the middle of the grate, adding in a few firelighters. Light the firelighters using matches or a taper, and leave the coals for about 40-45 minutes until they are glowing red and covered in a light grey ash.

Using a poker, garden rake or long-handled tongs, rake the coals over the grate's surface. If you need more than one temperature, rake some of the coals on top of each other so you have an area that has a double layer. This will be the hottest area, while the single layer has a more medium heat. This should remain hot for about 1 hour, but you can add a few more coals from time to time if necessary. The barbecue is considered hot when you can hold your hand about 12 cm (5 inches) above the coals for just a couple of seconds, medium-hot when you can manage 3–4 seconds and cool for 5–6 seconds. Alternatively, raise or lower the grill to alter the heat level.

lighting wood

Place a few small, dry twigs in the grate with a few firelighters. Add a good heap of wood chunks, light the firelighters and leave the wood to burn until it is glowing and ashen and no flames remain.

gas barbecues

A gas barbecue is highly practical as it can be lit in seconds and the temperature set with the twist of a knob. There are no hot coals to clear up afterwards and they are easy to clean. Most have a flat plate and a grill rack so you can cook every cut of meat or type of fish with ease. So whether cooking for two or a large group, dinner is quick and easy.

The cheapest gas barbecue is again 'table' shaped with legs and has gas burners rather than charcoal. These can have a lid and usually have both a grill and flat plate.

The slightly larger and more expensive gas barbecue on wheels come with a dome-shaped lid and often has an additional side shelf for stacking plates. They usually have a thermometer and some have a rotisserie attachment. The lid allows the barbecue to act like a conventional oven.

There is also an 'all bells and whistles' version, which is more like an outdoor kitchen for the true barbecue enthusiast. They often come in stainless steel, looking quite grand and will have all the mod cons.

Gas bottles are widely available from many garage outlets as well as hardware stores

and barbecue suppliers. A deposit is paid on the bottle and then it can be refilled as and when is necessary.

cooking on a barbecue

The most common cooking method on a barbecue is by the 'direct grilling method'. Here the food is cooked directly over a high heat (between 200–250°C/400–500°F) to give it that wonderful chargrilled flavour. This can be done on all types of barbecues and is usually for smaller pieces of meat, fish and vegetables that take less than 10 minutes to cook.

If using a charcoal barbecue, once the coals or wood are hot (they will have turned to glowing ash) and have been raked to their required position, spray the grill rack with oil away from the heat and replace over the coals. Leave for 5 minutes while the rack heats up so that the food is less likely to stick. Place the food on the rack and cook on both sides until ready.

For cooking on gas, preheat the barbecue about 15 minutes before you begin to cook. Allow to heat up and then turn the knob to the heat you require. Carefully brush or spray the grill rack or flat plate with oil and cook as per the recipe.

For larger pieces of meat and fish or fatty cuts of meat such as ribs or duck breast, the cooking method required is called 'indirect grilling'. This means that the food is cooked more slowly and at a lower temperature on a rack set over a roasting tin. This allows the fat from the meat to drip into a tray and not on to the flames or coals, which would cause too much smoke. This method requires a barbecue with a lid.

To cook by this method with coals or wood, rake the hot coals away from the centre of the grate to the edges, leaving a cool spot in the middle. The roasting tin and rack with the meat can now be set above the cool spot. You will need a lid for this method too.

You can also indirect grill easily on a gas barbecue, providing it has at least two burners. Preheat the barbecue to hot, then turn the burners down to medium. If you have two burners, then turn one off. If you have a three burners, turn the centre one off. Place the roasting tin with the rack and meat over the unlit burner, cover and cook as per the recipe.

To make a temporary lid, you can use the lid of a wok, which is ideal.

smoking

If the recipe requires smoking, the easiest and cheapest method is to make a smoking pouch using foil. Take a large rectangle of foil, about 60 cm (24 inches) long, and fold it in half crossways. Pre-soak a large handful of wood chips (which are readily available from most barbecue suppliers) in cold water for at least 30 minutes. Drain and place on one half of the foil. Fold the other side over and seal around the edges. Pierce ten or so holes into the foil with a knife. This can then be placed on the hot barbecue, either directly on the coals or wood, or directly on top of one of the gas burners beneath the actual grill rack. After a few minutes the wood will begin to smoke and you can then place the food on the oiled rack, cover with the lid and cook for the required time.

equipment

- Spray oil for spraying the food or the grill
- Long-handled tongs
- A pastry brush for basting
- Good-quality thick oven gloves
- Meat thermometer (ideal for testing if larger cuts are done)
- Matches or tapers
- Firelighters
- Sufficient fuel to last the evening
- A ridged grill pan (as an alternative to a flat plate if you have a charcoal barbecue)
- A good-quality wire brush for cleaning
- A grill basket for cooking fish or small items
- Metal or bamboo skewers for kebabs
- A torch or outdoor light for evening cooking

cleaning

Both charcoal and gas barbecues will need cleaning. Before cooking, use a wire brush to rub off any cooked-on bits of food from the grill rack. To avoid this at the time, though, the best time to clean the grill rack is directly after cooking while the rack is still hot. Use a wire brush to rub off as much of the cooked-on food as possible.

Always keep your barbecue dry when not in use, covered with a waterproof sheet during bad weather and through the winter.

Spraying the grill rack or flat plate with oil after cleaning will help to avoid rusting.

fire safety

• Always check that there are no weather warnings such as high winds if using charcoal or wood
• Always keep a fire extinguisher and fire blanket nearby just in case a fire does break out. Sand is the best method for putting out a ground fire, while salt will put out a grease fire on the rack

• Cook as close to the house or dining area as possible, to avoid carrying hot food long distances
• Place the barbecue in a sheltered spot where there is little or no wind to blow smoke and sparks and avoid areas with dry timbers or long, dry grass
• Place a portable barbecue on a flat, hard surface such as a patio and avoid cooking on a wooden deck
• Never leave hot coals or food, once cooking, unattended
• Do not wear open sandals when barbecuing: burns will be painful
• Always allow coals or wood to cool completely before safely and legally disposing of them. This can take up to 2 hours

food safety
• If you are marinating something for an hour or less, then it should be fine to do this in a cool place, but if in doubt, refrigerate it. If marinating overnight, always refrigerate and return to room temperature 1 hour before cooking
• If you are grilling vegetables to eat later, then try to get them to cool down as quickly as possible in a cool place, then chill in the refrigerator until required
• Always make sure that chicken and pork are thoroughly cooked through before eating. This can be done either by using a meat thermometer or by inserting a skewer into the

thickest part of the meat. If the juices run clear, the meat is cooked. If they are bloody, return to the grill and continue cooking
• Remember that young children, the elderly and pregnant women are particularly vulnerable to illness caused by unsafe foods, and the main way for food to become contaminated is by poor storage or the use of dirty utensils

taste tempters

prawn & bacon skewers

Serves **4**
Preparation time **15 minutes**,
  plus marinating
Cooking time **4–6 minutes**

4 **streaky bacon rashers**, rind
  removed
12 raw peeled large **prawns**,
  deveined but tails intact
12 **cherry tomatoes**
12 **basil leaves**
spray oil
salt and **black pepper**
1 **lemon**, to garnish

Soak 12 bamboo skewers in cold water for 30 minutes. Cut each bacon rasher into 3 pieces crossways, then run the back of a knife along the length of each piece to stretch them out thinly.

Wrap each prawn carefully with bacon and thread on to a soaked bamboo skewer with a tomato and basil leaf. Season each skewer with a little salt and pepper.

Spray the skewers with a little oil and cook on a hot barbecue for 2–3 minutes on each side until the prawns are cooked through. Squeeze with lemon juice and serve hot.

For date, goats' cheese & bacon canapés, take 4 bacon rashers and follow the method above to stretch them out thinly. Slit open 12 large Medjool dates and remove the pits. Place 1 teaspoon goats' cheese into each slit and then wrap each date with a piece of bacon. Thread on to soaked bamboo skewers and barbecue for 2–3 minutes on each side until the bacon is cooked.

yakitori chicken skewers

Serves **4**
Preparation time **15 minutes**,
  plus marinating
Cooking time **4–6 minutes**

3 tablespoons **Japanese soy
  sauce**
1½ tablespoons **sake** or **dry
  sherry**
1 tablespoon **caster sugar**
300 g (10 oz) skinless
  chicken thigh fillets, cut
  lengthways into 1 cm
  (½ inch) strips
75 g (3 oz) **Mayonnaise**
  (see page 158)
1 teaspoon **wasabi paste**

Combine the soy sauce, sake and sugar in a small
saucepan and heat gently to dissolve the sugar. Leave
to cool completely. Place the chicken in a shallow dish,
add the marinade and leave to marinate for at least
1 hour.

Soak 8 bamboo skewers in cold water for 30 minutes.
Mix the mayonnaise and wasabi paste together in a
bowl, then cover and set aside until required.

Thread the chicken on to the skewers and cook on
a hot barbecue for 2–3 minutes on each side until
cooked through. Serve with the wasabi mayonnaise
for dipping.

For teriyaki tuna, put 3 tablespoons soy sauce,
3 tablespoons sake, 2 tablespoons mirin (rice wine
seasoning) and 1 tablespoon caster sugar in a
saucepan and heat gently, stirring, until the sugar
dissolves. Leave to cool completely. Marinate
4 x 150 g (5 oz) tuna steaks in the sauce for
15 minutes. Drain the marinade back into the
saucepan and simmer gently for 2–3 minutes until
thickened. Meanwhile, barbecue the tuna fillets for
1 minute on each side and serve drizzled with the
teriyaki sauce.

spiced chicken wings

Serves **4**
Preparation time **10 minutes**,
  plus marinating
Cooking time **8—10 minutes**

8 large **chicken wings**
flat leaf parsley sprig,
  to garnish
lime wedges, to serve

Marinade
1 **garlic clove**
5 cm (2 inch) piece of **fresh
  root ginger,** peeled and
  chopped
juice and finely grated rind of
  2 limes
2 tablespoons **light soy sauce**
2 tablespoons **groundnut oil**
2 teaspoons **ground cinnamon**
1 teaspoon **ground turmeric**
2 tablespoons **clear honey**
salt

Yellow pepper dip
2 **yellow peppers**
2 tablespoons **natural yogurt**
1 tablespoon **dark soy sauce**
1 tablespoon chopped
  coriander
black pepper

Soak 8 bamboo skewers in cold water for 30 minutes.

Place the marinade ingredients in a blender or food processor and blend until smooth.

Arrange the chicken wings in a shallow dish, pour the marinade over and toss to cover. Cover and leave to marinate for 1—2 hours.

Put the peppers for the dip on a hot barbecue for 10 minutes, turning occasionally, until they are charred and blistered. Remove and place in a plastic bag, then seal and leave until cool. Peel off the skins and remove the seeds and white membrane. Put the flesh into a food processor or blender with the yogurt and blend until smooth. Pour into a bowl, season with soy sauce and pepper to taste and stir in the coriander. Cover and chill until needed.

Remove the chicken from the marinade, thread on to the skewers and cook on a hot barbecue for 4—5 minutes on each side, basting with the remaining marinade. Garnish with a parsley sprig, then serve with the dip and some lime wedges.

For spiced prawns, make the marinade as above, but reduce the honey to 1 teaspoon. Place in a bowl, add 20 raw peeled large prawns and stir to combine. Leave to marinate for 30 minutes. Thread the prawns on to soaked bamboo skewers and spray with oil. Barbecue the prawns for 2—3 minutes on each side and serve with lime wedges.

scallop & chorizo skewers

Serves **4**
Preparation time **10 minutes**,
  plus marinating
Cooking time **4—6 minutes**

12 **scallops**, white meat only
12 large **sage leaves**
150 g (5 oz) **chorizo**
  sausage, cut into 12 x 1 cm
  (½ inch) slices
2 tablespoons **extra virgin**
  olive oil
1 tablespoon **lemon juice**
1 **garlic clove**, crushed
salt and **black pepper**

Soak 12 small bamboo skewers in cold water for
30 minutes.

Wrap each scallop with a sage leaf and thread on to
the soaked bamboo skewers with a slice of the chorizo.
Mix the oil, lemon juice, garlic and salt and pepper
together and drizzle over the skewers. Marinate for
1 hour.

Cook the skewers on a hot barbecue for 2—3 minutes
on each side until the scallops are cooked though.
Serve at once.

For grilled scallops with pesto, take 12 scallops on
the half shell and season lightly with pepper. Drizzle
with a little oil and cook shell-side down on a hot
barbecue for 3—4 minutes until the scallops are
cooked (they will cook through the shell). Serve
topped with a spoonful of Pesto (see page 158).

ham & cheese quesadillas

Serves **4–8**
Preparation time **10 minutes**
Cooking time **4–6 minutes**

4 x 23 cm (9 inch) **flour
  tortillas**
200 g (7 oz) sliced **smoked
  ham**
2 **tomatoes**, thinly sliced
200 g (7 oz) **smoked cheese**,
  grated
2 tablespoons **coriander
  leaves**
salt and **black pepper**

Arrange 2 of the tortillas on a work surface and top with the ham, tomatoes, cheese, coriander and some salt and pepper. Top with the remaining tortillas, pressing down firmly. Cook one of the quesadillas on the flat plate of a hot gas barbecue for 2–3 minutes, turning halfway through, until each side is charred and crisp. (For a charcoal barbecue, use a preheated ridged grill pan instead.) Serve as below, then cook the second quesadilla.

Transfer the quesadillas to a board, cool for a second or two and then cut into wedges to serve.

For spinach & cheese quesadillas, beat together 250 g (8 oz) thawed, drained and chopped frozen spinach, 75 g (3 oz) crumbled feta cheese, 1 tablespoon grated Parmesan cheese, 1 tablespoon mascarpone cheese, a little grated nutmeg and some salt and pepper. Sandwich 4 flour tortillas with the spinach mixture and cook on a hot barbecue as in the method above. Serve in wedges.

marinated goats' cheese with pittas

Serves **4–6**
Preparation time **10 minutes**,
  plus marinating
Cooking time **2 minutes**

2 x 125 g (4 oz) **goats'
  cheese logs,** whole, or
  1 x 250 g (8 oz) **goats'
  cheese log,** sliced
75 ml (3 fl oz) **extra virgin
  olive oil**
1 tablespoon chopped **herbs**
  of choice
1 **red birds eye chilli,**
  deseeded and sliced
grated rind of 1 **lime**
4–6 large round **pitta breads**
extra virgin olive oil, for
  brushing
1½ teaspoons **zumac** or **dried
  thyme**
salt and **black pepper**

Arrange the goats' cheese in a shallow ceramic dish.
Combine the oil, herbs, chilli, lime rind and some salt
and pepper and pour over the cheese. Leave to
marinate for 1 hour.

Place the pitta breads on a board. Brush the tops with
oil and season with the zumac, salt and pepper. Toast,
spice side up, on a hot barbecue for 1 minute, then
flip and cook the spiced side for 1 minute until crisp.

Cut the bread into wedges and serve with the goats'
cheese and its marinade.

For garlic butter pittas, melt 50 g (2 oz) butter in
a small saucepan with 1 crushed garlic clove and a
little black pepper. Barbecue 4 plain pitta breads for
1 minute on each side until charred and crisp. Brush
the pittas with the garlic butter and serve in wedges.

baba ganoush with grilled tortillas

Serves **6**
Preparation time **10 minutes**,
   plus cooling and marinating
Cooking time **22—27 minutes**

1 **aubergine**, about 500 g
   (1 lb)
1 **garlic clove**, crushed
1 tablespoon **lemon juice**
1 tablespoon chopped
   coriander
2 teaspoons **tahini**
pinch of **cayenne pepper**
4 x 23 cm (9 inch) **flour**
   tortillas
olive oil, for brushing
salt and **black pepper**

Wipe the aubergine, prick it all over with a fork and cook on a hot barbecue for 20—25 minutes, turning frequently, until the flesh feels soft and the skin is blackened. Set aside until cool enough to handle.

Peel and discard the skin, then mash the flesh and strain in a sieve to extract all the excess liquid. Transfer the flesh to a blender or food processor, add the garlic, lemon juice, coriander, tahini, cayenne and some salt and pepper and blend until fairly smooth. Transfer to a bowl, cover and leave to marinate for several hours for the flavours to develop.

Brush the tortillas lightly with a little oil and toast on the barbecue for 1 minute on each side. Cut into strips and serve with the dip.

For grilled aubergine, tomato & olive dip, cut a medium aubergine crossways into 5 mm (¼ inch) thick slices, brush with oil and season with salt and black pepper. Cook on a hot barbecue for 2–3 minutes each side until charred and tender. Leave to cool and dice finely. Toss the aubergine with 1 finely chopped tomato, 50 g (2 oz) chopped pitted black olives, 1 crushed garlic clove, 1 tablespoon chopped fresh coriander, 2 tablespoons extra virgin olive oil and a squeeze of lemon juice. Serve with 4 tortillas, toasted as above.

bresaola bruschetta

Serves **6**
Preparation time **5 minutes**
Cooking time **2 minutes**

6 slices of **sourdough bread**
3 ripe **tomatoes**
4 tablespoons **Smoked Garlic Oil** (see page 196)
6 slices of **bresaola** or **prosciutto**
black pepper

Toast the bread on a medium barbecue for 1 minute on each side until charred. Remove.

Cut the tomatoes in half and rub them all over one side of the charred bread slices, then drizzle generously with the garlic oil.

Place the slices tomato side up on a platter and top each one with the bresaola and some pepper. Serve drizzled with a little extra garlic oil.

For tomato bruschetta, combine 3 diced vine-ripened tomatoes, 1 crushed garlic clove, 1 tablespoon shredded basil, 1 tablespoon extra virgin olive oil and some salt and pepper. Toast 6 slices of sourdough bread following the method above and serve topped with the tomato mixture.

melon & parma ham salad

Serves **4–6**
Preparation time **5 minutes**

1 small **Charentais melon**,
  halved and deseeded
1 small **Galia** or **Ogen melon**,
  halved and deseeded
12 thin slices of **Parma ham**
mint sprigs, to garnish

Dressing
75 g (3 oz) **dolcelatte cheese**
2 tablespoons **lemon juice**
5 tablespoons **milk**
2 tablespoons chopped **mint**
salt and **black pepper**

Start by making the dressing. Put the dolcelatte and lemon juice in a small bowl and mash to a paste, using a fork. Stir in the milk and mint and add salt and pepper to taste.

Slice the melons into thin wedges. Alternatively, slice just 1 of the melons and use a melon baller to scoop out the flesh of the other.

Arrange the melon on individual serving plates with the slices of Parma ham. Spoon the dressing over and around the melon, garnish with mint and serve immediately.

For roasted pepper, chilli & basil salad, cook 3 red peppers on a hot barbecue for about 15 minutes, turning them every 3–4 minutes until evenly charred. Meanwhile, cook 2 large green chillies in the same way for 4–5 minutes, turning halfway through. Transfer the peppers and chillies to a plastic bag, seal and leave to cool, then peel and deseed them. Put in a bowl and dress with 3 tablespoons extra virgin olive oil, 2 teaspoons sherry vinegar, 1 crushed garlic clove, salt and pepper and serve garnished with basil leaves.

cheesy garlic bread

Serves **4**
Preparation time **5 minutes**
Cooking time **10 minutes**

1 small **French stick**
75 ml (3 fl oz) **extra virgin olive oil**
1 **garlic clove**, crushed
2 teaspoons chopped **thyme**
125 g (4 oz) **buffalo mozzarella cheese**, thinly sliced
salt and **black pepper**

Cut 20 slices in the French stick without going all the way through. Combine the oil, garlic, thyme and salt and pepper in a bowl and brush the mixture all over the cut sides and the top of the bread.

Place a slice of mozzarella in between each slice of bread. Place the stick on a double layer of foil and seal loosely. Cook on a medium-hot barbecue for 5 minutes, then open the foil out (using oven gloves, as the foil will be hot) and cook for a further 5 minutes. Serve hot.

For bread, tomato & mozzarella skewers, cut a small French stick into 2.5 cm (1 inch) cubes and thread on to 4–6 pre-soaked large bamboo skewers, alternating with a cube of diced mozzarella and a cherry tomato. Place in a ceramic dish. Mix 4 tablespoons extra virgin olive oil with 1 tablespoon chopped mixed herbs and some salt and pepper. Pour the mixture over the skewers and leave to marinate for 1 hour. Cook on a medium-hot barbecue for 2–3 minutes until the cheese starts to melt.

prosciutto & asparagus parcels

Serves **4**
Preparation time **10 minutes**
Cooking time **8–10 minutes**

24 **asparagus spears**,
   trimmed
4 slices of **prosciutto**
2 Spanish **piquillo peppers**,
   drained and sliced
4 **thyme sprigs**
4 **anchovy fillets in oil**,
   drained
salt and **black pepper**
Aïoli (see page 122), to serve

Blanch the asparagus spears in lightly salted boiling water for 2 minutes. Drain well and refresh under cold water. Pat dry.

Lay a slice of prosciutto flat on a board and top with 3 asparagus spears, a slice of pepper, a thyme sprig, an anchovy fillet and 3 more asparagus spears. Roll up into a parcel and secure with cooking string. Repeat to make 4 parcels.

Cook on a medium barbecue for 6–8 minutes, turning frequently, until evenly charred and tender. Serve the parcels with aïoli.

For grilled asparagus 'soldiers', brush 20 large asparagus spears with a little oil, season and cook on a hot barbecue for 3–4 minutes, turning halfway through, until charred and tender. Serve 5 asparagus 'soldiers' per person, each with a soft-boiled egg to dip them into.

lemon grass chicken kebabs

Serves **6**

Preparation time **20 minutes**, plus marinating

Cooking time **8 minutes**

500 g (1 lb) skinless **chicken thigh fillets**, cut into thin strips

2 **garlic cloves**, crushed

2 teaspoons peeled and grated **fresh root ginger**

1 **red birds eye chilli**, deseeded and finely chopped

grated rind of 1 **lime**

2 tablespoons **light soy sauce**

1 tablespoon **sesame oil**

1 teaspoon **caster sugar**

¼ teaspoon **black pepper**

6 large **lemon grass stalks**

Place the chicken in a shallow nonmetallic dish. Combine all the remaining ingredients except for the lemon grass stalks and leave to marinate for 1 hour.

Peel and discard a few of the outer layers of the lemon grass stalks so that they are a little finer. Cut the thinner end into a point and thread the marinated chicken on to each stalk at this end, zig-zagging backwards and forwards as you go. Cook on a hot barbecue for 3–4 minutes on each side, brushing with the marinade halfway through. Serve hot.

For chicken yogurt skewers, combine 150 g (5 oz) Greek yogurt with 2 teaspoons ground coriander, 1 teaspoon each ground cumin and cinnamon, 2 crushed garlic cloves, grated rind and juice of ½ lemon, 1 teaspoon clear honey and some salt and pepper. Prepare 500 g (1 lb) chicken thigh fillets following the method above and marinate them in the yogurt mix for 1 hour. Thread on to 6 metal skewers and grill as above. Serve with a rocket salad.

steak & ribs

herbed lamb with fig salad

Serves **4**

Preparation time **15 minutes**, plus marinating

Cooking time **4—6 minutes**

100 ml (3½ fl oz) **extra virgin olive oil**

1 quantity **Rosemary, Coriander & Lemon Rub** (see page 192)

1 **garlic clove**, crushed

12 **lamb cutlets**

125 g (4 oz) **wild rocket**

4 **figs**, sliced

75 g (3 oz) pitted **black olives**, halved

2—3 teaspoons **lemon juice**, to taste

salt and **black pepper**

Tahini Sauce, to serve (see page 98)

Put 2 tablespoons of the oil, the Rosemary, Coriander & Lemon Rub, the garlic and some salt and pepper in a zip-lock bag. Add the lamb, toss well and seal the bag. Leave to marinate in a cool place for 1—4 hours.

Remove the lamb from the marinade and pat dry. Cook on a hot barbecue for 2—3 minutes on each side, then wrap loosely with foil and set aside for 5 minutes.

Meanwhile, make the salad. Put the rocket, figs and olives in a large bowl and mix well. Whisk together the remaining oil and 2—3 teaspoons lemon juice with some salt and pepper. Add to the salad and stir to coat the leaves. Serve with the lamb and some Tahini Sauce.

For lamb steaks with mint butter, combine 125 g (4 oz) softened butter with 2 tablespoons chopped mint and some black pepper. Roll into a log, wrap in foil and chill for 1 hour. Season 4 x 200 g (7 oz) lamb leg steaks and cook on a hot barbecue for 3—4 minutes on each side. Rest and serve topped with slices of the mint butter.

barbecued spare ribs

Serves **4**

Preparation time **20 minutes**, plus marinating

Cooking time **1 hour 10 minutes–1 hour 25 minutes**

1 kg (2 lb) **pork spare rib rack**

1 tablespoon **olive oil**, plus extra for brushing

4 tablespoons **Smoky Barbecue Rub** (see page 194)

Barbecue sauce

250 ml (8 fl oz) **tomato purée**

125 ml (4 fl oz) **treacle**

75 ml (3 fl oz) **maple syrup**

75 ml (3 fl oz) **white wine vinegar**

2 tablespoons **Worcestershire sauce**

1 tablespoon **Dijon mustard**

1 teaspoon **garlic powder**

¼ teaspoon **smoked paprika**

salt and **black pepper**

Place the ribs in a large, shallow nonmetallic dish. Mix the oil and barbecue rub together and then rub this all over the ribs. Cover and leave to marinate overnight in the refrigerator.

Meanwhile, make the barbecue sauce. Place all the ingredients in a saucepan and heat gently until boiling. Simmer gently for 10–15 minutes until the sauce has thickened slightly, then set aside to cool.

Remove the ribs from the dish, brush with a little extra oil and cook on a medium barbecue for 10 minutes on each side. Brush liberally with the barbecue sauce and transfer to a rack set in a roasting tin.

Cook by indirect grilling (see page 12) for a further 25–30 minutes on each side, basting frequently with more sauce, until charred and tender. Serve with a green salad, if liked.

For barbecued mustard & honey chicken wings, brush 12 large chicken wings with a little oil, season with salt and pepper and cook on a medium barbecue for 15 minutes on each side. Mix 2 tablespoons dark soy sauce with 2 teaspoons Dijon mustard and 1 teaspoon clear honey. Brush this mixture over the wings and cook for a final 1–2 minutes on each side until glazed.

steaks with chimichurri sauce

Serves **4**
Preparation time **20 minutes**
Cooking time **6–8 minutes**

4 **rib eye steaks**, about 200 g
 (7 oz) each
extra virgin olive oil, for
 brushing
salt and **black pepper**

Chimichurri sauce
bunch of **coriander**
bunch of **parsley**
2 teaspoons **dried oregano**
2 **garlic cloves**, chopped
1 teaspoon **smoked paprika**
150 ml (¼ pint) **extra virgin
 olive oil**
2 tablespoons **red wine
 vinegar**

Salsa
1 **avocado**, peeled, pitted
 and diced
12 **cherry tomatoes**, halved
2 **red birds eye chillies**,
 deseeded and finely
 chopped
2 tablespoons **coriander
 leaves**
juice of ½ **lime**

Place all the chimichurri sauce ingredients in a food processor or blender and blend until fairly smooth. Season to taste and set aside until required.

Brush the steaks with a little oil and season liberally with salt and pepper. Cook on a hot barbecue for 3–4 minutes on each side or until cooked to your liking. Set aside to rest for 3 minutes.

Meanwhile, make the salsa. Put the avocado, tomatoes, chilli, coriander, lime juice and some salt and pepper in a bowl and mix well.

Serve the steaks topped with the salsa and drizzled with the chimichurri sauce.

For steaks with salsa verde, start by making the sauce. Purée a bunch of parsley with ½ bunch each of mint, basil and chives, a crushed garlic clove, 1 tablespoon pitted green olives, 1 tablespoon capers, 2 anchovy fillets, 1 teaspoon Dijon mustard, 2 teaspoons white wine vinegar, 150 ml (¼ pint) extra virgin olive oil and some salt and pepper. Following the method above, cook 4 rib eye steaks to your liking. Serve with the salsa verde.

fillet steak with tapenade sauce

Serves **4**
Preparation time **8 minutes**
Cooking time **14–17 minutes**

50 g (2 oz) **butter**
4 **shallots**, finely chopped
1 tablespoon **wholegrain
mustard**
1 teaspoon **Dijon mustard**
2 tablespoons **ready-made
or homemade black olive
tapenade** (see below)
150 ml (¼ pint) **cider**
4 thick **fillet steaks**, about
200 g (7 oz) each
2 tablespoons coarsely
ground **black peppercorns**
2 tablespoons **crème fraîche**
2 tablespoons chopped
tarragon
salt and **black pepper**

Heat the butter in a frying pan until it has melted and is beginning to froth. Add the shallots and fry gently for 5–6 minutes until softened. Add the wholegrain and Dijon mustards and the tapenade and pour in the cider. Simmer gently for 2 minutes, then remove from the heat.

Press the fillet steaks into the black pepper. Cook on a hot barbecue for 3–4 minutes on each side or until cooked to your liking. Rest on warm serving plates while finishing off the tapenade.

Stir the crème fraîche and tarragon into the tapenade, season to taste with salt and pepper and gently warm the sauce without letting it boil. Pour a little of the sauce over each fillet steak and serve immediately with steamed asparagus, homemade chips and a dish of mustardy mayonnaise.

For homemade tapenade sauce, combine 125 g (4 oz) pitted black olives, 2 drained anchovy fillets, 2 crushed garlic cloves, 2 tablespoons drained capers, 1 teaspoon Dijon mustard, 4 tablespoons extra virgin olive oil and a squeeze of lemon juice in a food processor or blender and blend until smooth. Season to taste.

steaks with garlic-herb butter

Serves **4**
Preparation time **10 minutes**,
   plus chilling
Cooking time **10 minutes**

4 **T-bone steaks**, about
   500 g (1 lb) each
1½ tablespoons chopped
   thyme
2 tablespoons **extra virgin**
   olive oil
salt and **black pepper**

Garlic & parsley butter
125 g (4 oz) **butter**, softened
1 **garlic clove**, crushed
2 tablespoons drained **capers**
1 tablespoon chopped
   parsley

Put the ingredients for the butter in a bowl and season to taste. Shape into a log, wrap in clingfilm and chill until required. Cut into slices.

Season the steaks with salt, pepper and thyme and rub with oil. Cook on a hot barbecue for 5 minutes on each side, then wrap loosely in foil and set aside to rest for 5 minutes. Serve topped with the butter.

For steaks with grilled mushrooms, season and oil 4 trimmed large field mushrooms. Cook on a hot barbecue for 5–6 minutes on each side until tender. Meanwhile, following the method above, cook 4 T-bone steaks to your liking. Rest and serve with the mushrooms, some chopped parsley, a squeeze of lemon juice and a generous dash of extra virgin olive oil.

hoisin ribs

Serves **4**
Preparation time **25 minutes**
Cooking time **65–70 minutes**

1 kg (2 lb) **pork spare rib rack**
4 tablespoons **white wine vinegar**
sliced **spring onions**, to garnish

Hoisin barbecue sauce
50 ml (2 fl oz) **hoisin sauce**
50 ml (2 fl oz) **tomato ketchup**
2 tablespoons **white wine vinegar**
2 tablespoons **dark soy sauce**
2 tablespoons **clear honey**
1 large **garlic clove**, crushed
1 teaspoon freshly peeled and grated **fresh root ginger**
1 teaspoon **sesame oil**
½ teaspoon **Chinese five-spice powder**

Place the ribs in a large saucepan with the vinegar and add enough water to cover by a good 5 cm (2 inches). Bring to the boil and simmer for 20 minutes. Drain the ribs and dry on kitchen paper. Transfer to a bowl.

Meanwhile, place all the sauce ingredients in a saucepan and bring just to the boil. Simmer gently for 6–8 minutes until thickened slightly.

Brush the ribs with the marinade and, using the indirect grilling method (see page 12), cook on a medium barbecue for 45–50 minutes, basting and turning frequently until the ribs are glazed and tender. Serve with steamed rice.

For hoisin salmon steaks, make the sauce as above and leave to cool. Brush 4 x 200 g (7 oz) salmon steaks with a little of the sauce and cook on a medium barbecue for 3–4 minutes on each side. Serve with a crisp green salad.

rum & maple pork belly

Serves **6**

Preparation time **5 minutes**, plus marinating

Cooking time **1 hour 40 minutes–1 hour 50 minutes**

1 kg (2 lb) piece of **pork belly**, skin and ribs removed, or same weight **pork belly rashers**

1 tablespoon **olive oil**

2–4 tablespoons **jerk spice seasoning**

Rum & maple glaze

125 ml (4 fl oz) **maple syrup**

100 g (3½ oz) **light brown soft sugar**

4 tablespoons **dark rum**

juice of 1 **orange**

2 tablespoons **red wine vinegar**

½ teaspoon **ground cinnamon**

salt and **pepper**

Place the pork belly in a ceramic dish and brush with oil. Rub the jerk seasoning all over the pork and marinate overnight in the refrigerator. Return to room temperature 1 hour before cooking and remove from the marinade.

Cook the pork belly on a hot barbecue for 10 minutes each side until browned, then transfer to a rack set over a roasting tin. Cook by indirect grilling method (see page 12) for 1 hour.

Meanwhile, make the glaze. Place all the ingredients in a saucepan and heat gently until the sugar is dissolved. Simmer gently for 10 minutes until the glaze is thick and syrup-like.

Brush the pork belly with the glaze and cook for a further 10–15 minutes each side until it is fully glazed and meltingly tender.

For new potato salad, to serve as an accompaniment, cook 750 g (1½ lb) scrubbed new potatoes until tender. Drain well, mash very lightly to break the potatoes up a little and stir in 4 tablespoons good-quality mayonnaise, 4 trimmed and finely sliced spring onions, 2 tablespoons snipped chives, 1 tablespoon white wine vinegar, 2 teaspoons wholegrain mustard and some salt and pepper. Leave to cool.

fennel pork with tarragon butter

Serves **4**
Preparation time **5 minutes**,
  plus chilling
Cooking time **8—10 minutes**

4 **pork loin chops**, about
  250 g (8 oz) each
1 tablespoon **olive oil**
2 tablespoons **Fennel Rub**
  (see page 192)
lemon wedges, to serve

Tarragon butter
125 g (4 oz) **butter**
2 tablespoons chopped
  tarragon
salt and **black pepper**

Brush the pork chops with oil, rub in the spice mixture and then place in a shallow dish. Leave to marinate in a cool place for 2 hours.

Meanwhile, beat the butter, tarragon and some pepper together until well blended. Roll into a log and wrap in clingfilm, then chill until required.

Cook the steaks on a hot barbecue for 4—5 minutes on each side, then wrap loosely in foil and set aside to rest for 5 minutes. Cut the butter into slices and serve on top of the steaks, with lemon wedges alongside.

For chargrilled salmon with tarragon butter, lightly season 4 x 200 g (7 oz) salmon fillets, brush with oil and barbecue on a high heat for 3—4 minutes on each side. Rest briefly and serve topped with slices of tarragon butter, following the recipe above.

prosciutto-wrapped beef

Serves **8**
Preparation time **30 minutes**
Cooking time **25 minutes**,
  plus resting

2 tablespoons chopped
  thyme
grated rind of 2 **lemons**
4 tablespoons **extra virgin
  olive oil**
2 **beef eye fillets**, about
  750 g (1½ lb) each
12 large slices of **prosciutto**
4 large **potatoes**, such as
  Desiree, about 1.25 kg
  (2.5 lb) total weight
salt and **black pepper**

Mix the thyme, lemon rind, 2 tablespoons of the oil and some salt and pepper together and rub it all over the beef fillet. Wrap the prosciutto around the beef to flavour it and keep it moist, and secure in place with cooking string.

Cook on the flat plate of a hot gas barbecue for 25 minutes, turning frequently (or use the indirect grilling method for a charcoal barbecue). Remove the beef, wrap in a double layer of foil and set aside to rest for 20 minutes.

Meanwhile, cut the potatoes lengthways into 1 cm (½ inch) thick slices and parboil for 5 minutes. Drain well, brush with the remaining oil and season with salt and pepper. Cook the potato slices on the grill rack for 3—4 minutes on each side until charred and tender.

Slice the beef and serve with the potatoes and a spinach salad (see below).

For spinach salad, to serve as an accompaniment, wash and drain 125 g (4 oz) baby spinach leaves and place in a bowl. Whisk together 2 tablespoons extra virgin olive oil, 2 teaspoons red wine vinegar, a pinch of caster sugar and some salt and pepper. Pour the dressing over the salad, toss well and serve.

moroccan chicken & salad

Serves: **4–6**
Preparation time **15 minutes**,
    plus marinating
Cooking time **12–16 minutes**

4 **chicken breast fillets** with
    skin, about 250 g (8 oz) each
2 tablespoons **pomegranate**
    molasses (or 2 tablespoons
    honey mixed with
    1 teaspoon **lemon juice**)
1 tablespoon **extra virgin**
    olive oil
2 teaspoons **zumac** or **dried**
    thyme
salt and **black pepper**

Moroccan salad
1 small **aubergine**
2 tablespoons **extra virgin**
    olive oil
2 **flatbreads**
250 g (8 oz) **cherry**
    tomatoes, quartered
1 **Lebanese cucumber**, diced
75 g (3 oz) pitted **black**
    olives, chopped
½ bunch each **mint, coriander**
    and **parsley leaves**
1 **pomegranate**, peeled
juice of ½ **lemon**
1 teaspoon **caster sugar**

Score the skin side of each chicken breast several times and place in a bowl. Add the pomegranate molasses, oil, zumac and a generous sprinkling of salt and pepper. Rub into the chicken and leave to marinate in a cool place for 1 hour.

Remove the chicken from the marinade, reserving the juices, and cook on a medium-hot barbecue for 6–8 minutes on each side until charred and cooked through. Set aside to rest for 5 minutes.

Heat the reserved marinade juices in a small pan until boiling and reduced slightly. Brush over the cooked chicken to glaze.

Meanwhile, make the salad. Cut the aubergine crossways into 5 mm (¼ inch) thick slices. Brush with a little of the oil and cook on a hot barbecue for 1–2 minutes each side. Toast the flatbreads on the barbecue for 30 seconds or so on each side until crisp, then crumble into a large bowl. Add the tomatoes, cucumber, olives, herbs and pomegranate seeds. Whisk the remaining oil, lemon juice, sugar and a little salt and pepper and add to the salad. Toss well and serve with the chicken.

For pomegranate chicken wings, follow the above recipe, replacing the chicken breast with 12 large wings. Marinate for 1 hour and cook on a medium-hot barbecue for 10–12 minutes on each side. Cool for 5 minutes before serving with a crisp green salad.

spatchcocked citrus chicken

Serves **4**
Preparation time **15 minutes**
Cooking time **40 minutes**

1.5 kg (3 lb) **chicken**
2 tablespoons **extra virgin olive oil**
salt and **black pepper**

Grilled lemon dressing
3 **lemons**, halved
spray oil
1 **garlic clove**, crushed
75 ml (3 fl oz) **extra virgin olive oil**
pinch of **caster sugar**
1 large **red chilli**, deseeded and finely chopped
2 tablespoons chopped **parsley**

Ask your butcher to spatchcock the chicken for you, or do it yourself if you know how.

Season the chicken with salt and pepper and rub with the oil. Thread two metal skewers through the bird diagonally (from wing tip to drumstick) to keep flat. Cook on a hot barbecue, breast-side down, for 5 minutes, then lower the heat to medium and cook, covered, for 15 minutes. Turn the chicken over and cook for a further 20 minutes. Set aside to rest for 10 minutes.

Meanwhile, spray the cut face of the lemon halves with a little oil and place them, cut-side down, on a hot barbecue. Cook for 10 minutes, turning frequently, until charred and softened. Set aside to cool.

Squeeze the lemon juice from two lemon halves into a bowl and stir in the garlic, oil, sugar, chilli, parsley and salt and pepper to taste.

Transfer the cooked bird to a board, cut into large pieces using a big knife and place on a warmed platter. Pour the dressing over it and serve garnished with some chilli and parsley and the remaining lemon halves.

For watercress, lambs lettuce & almond salad, to serve as an accompaniment, toast 100 g (3½ oz) blanched almonds in a preheated oven, 190°C (375°F), Gas Mark 6, for 5–6 minutes until evenly browned. Set aside to cool. Combine 50 g (2 oz) watercress leaves, 50 g (2 oz) lambs lettuce, the almonds and 75 g (3 oz) sultanas in a bowl. Drizzle a little oil and a dash of balsamic vinegar over, season with salt and pepper and stir. Serve with the chicken.

lamb with beetroot & feta salad

Serves **4**

Preparation time **15 minutes**,
  plus marinating

Cooking time **40–45 minutes**

2 **lamb back loins**, about
  250 g (8 oz) each
1 tablespoon **extra virgin
  olive oil**
1 tablespoon **dried oregano**
500 g (1 lb) small **beetroot**
200 g (7 oz) **green beans**,
  trimmed
125 g (4 oz) **feta cheese**
100 g (3½ oz) **baby spinach
  leaves**
100 g (3½ oz) **walnuts**,
  toasted
salt and **black pepper**

**Walnut oil & raspberry
dressing**
3 tablespoons **walnut oil**
2–3 teaspoons **raspberry
  vinegar**
2 teaspoons **wholegrain
  mustard**

Brush the lamb loins with the oil and rub with the oregano and some salt and pepper. Set aside to marinate for 1 hour.

Meanwhile, place the beetroot in a saucepan of cold water, bring to the boil and cook for 20 minutes until just tender. Drain well, cut into wedges and place in a bowl. Add a little oil and thread on to 2 metal skewers. Cook on a hot barbecue for 6–8 minutes on each side until lightly charred. Return to the bowl.

Blanch the beans in lightly salted boiling water for 3 minutes. Drain, refresh under cold water and dry well. Add to the beetroot with the feta, spinach and walnuts.

Whisk the dressing ingredients and some salt and pepper together in a small bowl.

Cook the lamb on a hot barbecue for 4–5 minutes on each side, then set aside to rest briefly. Serve in slices with the salad, drizzled with the dressing.

For chargrilled loin chops with mint dressing, lightly season 8 x 125 g (4 oz) loin chops, brush with a little oil and cook on a hot barbecue for 3–4 minutes on each side. Rest briefly. Meanwhile, whisk together 2 tablespoons chopped mint, 5 tablespoons white wine vinegar, 2 tablespoons extra virgin olive oil, 2 teaspoons caster sugar and some salt and pepper. Drizzle over the chops and serve with a simple green salad.

steak with mustardy chips

Serves **4**
Preparation time **10 minutes**
Cooking time **20 minutes**

500 g (1 lb) **potatoes**,
   scrubbed
3 tablespoons **olive oil**
1 **egg white**
1 teaspoon **wholegrain
   mustard**
½ teaspoon **ground turmeric**
250 g (8 oz) **cherry tomatoes**
250 g (8 oz) **closed cup
   mushrooms**, trimmed
4 thick-cut **sirloin steaks**,
   about 200 g (7 oz) each,
   trimmed
black pepper

Parboil the potatoes for 5 minutes, then drain. Cut
in half lengthways, then cut into chunky wedges. Put
1 tablespoon of the oil in a bowl, add the egg white,
mustard, turmeric and a little pepper and fork together
until the egg white is slightly frothy. Add the potatoes
and toss well.

Arrange the potato wedges in a single layer on the
flat plate of a hot gas barbecue or in a ridged pan on
a charcoal barbecue and cook for 10 minutes. Add
the tomatoes and cook for 5 more minutes or until the
chips are golden and the tomato skins just beginning
to split.

Meanwhile, brush the mushrooms and steaks
with the remaining oil and sprinkle the steaks with
a little pepper. Cook the steaks on the barbecue for
3—4 minutes on each side, or until cooked to your
liking. Set aside to rest for 5 minutes while cooking
the mushrooms.

Transfer the steak, chips and vegetables to serving
plates and serve immediately.

For watercress salad, to serve as an accompaniment,
combine 125 g (4 oz) watercress leaves with 50 g
(2 oz) frisée leaves in a large bowl and add 50 g
(2 oz) toasted walnuts. Mix together 2 teaspoons
white wine vinegar, 2 teaspoons wholegrain mustard,
½ teaspoon caster sugar and some salt and pepper
in a bowl and whisk in 3 tablespoons walnut oil. Pour
over the salad and stir to combine.

kebabs, burgers & hot dogs

hot dogs with barbecue sauce

Serves **4**
Preparation time **10 minutes**
Cooking time **15–20 minutes**

2 large **onions**, sliced
2 tablespoons **extra virgin olive oil**
1 tablespoon chopped **thyme**
4 large **pork sausages**
4 **hot dog rolls**, halved
a little **butter**
4 tablespoons **Barbecue Sauce** (see page 46)
salt and **black pepper**

Toss the onions with the oil, thyme, salt and pepper, then cook on the flat plate of a hot gas barbecue for 15–20 minutes until soft and golden. (For a charcoal barbecue, use a preheated ridged grill pan instead.)

Meanwhile, cook the sausages on the barbecue until lightly charred and cooked through, about 10 minutes.

Butter the bread rolls and fill with the sausages, onions and a tablespoon of barbecue sauce.

For mustard & pickle dogs, cook the sausages and onions as in the recipe above. Serve in 4 hot dog rolls topped with 2 medium dill pickles, diced, and a drizzle of classic American mustard.

chicken & mozzarella skewers

Serves **4**
Preparation time **25 minutes**
Cooking time **16 minutes**

8 small boneless **chicken thigh fillets**, skinned
2 **bocconcini balls** (baby mozzarellas), quartered
8 large **basil leaves**
8 large slices of **prosciutto**
2 small **lemons**, halved
salt and **black pepper**

Lay the chicken thighs flat with the boned side facing upwards. Season each one with a little salt and pepper. Place one-quarter of a bocconcini and a basil leaf in the centre of each one and roll the chicken up to enclose the filling. Wrap each thigh in a slice of prosciutto and thread on to 8 metal skewers, allowing 2 skewers per 2 parcels (making them easy to turn).

Cook the skewers on the flat plate of a hot gas barbecue for 8 minutes on each side until the mozzarella starts to ooze. (For a charcoal barbecue, cook directly on the rack.) Wrap in foil and set aside to rest for 5 minutes. Take care when handling the skewers as they will be very hot.

Meanwhile, cook the lemon halves, cut-side down, for 5 minutes until charred and tender.

Serve the skewers drizzled with the lemon juice.

For rocket & Parmesan salad, to serve as an accompaniment, put 125 g (4 oz) baby rocket leaves in a bowl and season lightly with salt and pepper. Whisk together 2 tablespoons extra virgin olive oil, 1 teaspoon balsamic vinegar and some salt and pepper. Drizzle a little of the dressing over the rocket, toss well and serve scattered with 15 g (½ oz) shaved Parmesan.

classic hamburger

Serves **4**
Preparation time **10 minutes**,
  plus chilling
Cooking time **10–12 minutes**

500 g (1 lb) **rib eye steak**,
  minced
250 g (8 oz) skinless **pork
  belly**, minced
1 **onion**, finely chopped
1 teaspoon **Worcestershire
  sauce**
2 tablespoons drained **capers**
olive oil, for brushing
4 **hamburger buns**, halved
2 tablespoons **mustard**
100 g (3½ oz) shredded
  lettuce leaves
2 **tomatoes**, sliced
2 **dill pickles**, sliced
salt and **black pepper**

Put the beef and pork mince in a bowl with the onion,
Worcestershire sauce, capers, salt and pepper. Mix
together well, using your hands. Divide the mixture into
quarters and shape into 4 even-sized patties. Chill for
30 minutes.

Brush the patties with oil and cook on a hot barbecue
for 5–6 minutes on each side until lightly charred on
the outside while just cooked through inside.

Meanwhile, toast the buns on the barbecue for
1 minute on each side.

Spread the insides of the buns with a little mustard,
fill with the shredded lettuce, patties, tomato slices
and dill pickles.

For beef burgers with grilled onions, follow the
recipe above, omitting the pork belly and using
750 g (1½ lb) minced steak. Combine the beef with
1 finely chopped onion, 4 finely chopped anchovies,
2 tablespoons chopped parsley and some salt and
pepper. Shape into patties, cook and served topped
with some browned onions (see page 72).

cheeseburger

Serves **4**
Preparation time **15 minutes**,
    plus chilling
Cooking time **10–12 minutes**

750 g (1½ lb) **rib eye steak**,
    minced
1 **onion**, finely chopped
1 **garlic clove**, crushed
2 teaspoons chopped **thyme**
olive oil, for brushing
125 g (4 oz) **Cheddar
    cheese**, grated
4 **burger buns**, halved
4 large **butter lettuce leaves**
2 **tomatoes**, sliced
salt and **black pepper**

Put the beef, onion, garlic, thyme and some salt and
pepper in a bowl. Using your hands, work them
together until evenly combined and slightly sticky.
Divide the mixture into quarters and shape into
4 even-sized patties. Chill for 30 minutes.

Brush the patties with a little oil and cook on a hot
barbecue for 5–6 minutes on each side until cooked
through and lightly charred on the outside. Top the
burgers with cheese and place under a hot grill for
30 seconds until melted.

Meanwhile, toast the buns on the barbecue for
1 minute on the cut side.

Fill each bun with the lettuce leaves, cheese-topped
patties and tomato slices.

For Stilton-stuffed burgers, cut 50 g (2 oz) Stilton
cheese into 4 pieces. Make 4 patties following the
recipe above, shaping each one around a piece of
Stilton, so that it is well hidden in the centre. Cook
as above and serve in 4 toasted wholemeal buns
with a little watercress and some mayonnaise.

sicilian burgers

Serves **4**

Preparation time **20 minutes**, plus chilling

Cooking time **12—14 minutes**

1 tablespoon **olive oil**

1 **red onion**, finely chopped

3 **garlic cloves**, finely chopped

625 g (1¼ lb) good-quality **coarsely minced beef**

2 tablespoons chopped **basil**

2 tablespoons chopped **marjoram**

2 tablespoons chopped **oregano**

50 g (2 oz) freshly grated **Parmesan cheese**

75 g (3 oz) **sun-dried tomatoes**, finely chopped

75 g (3 oz) **black olives**, finely chopped

a little **olive oil**, for brushing

2 soft **focaccia rolls**, quartered, then halved

Mayonnaise (see page 158), flavoured with 4 tablespoons chopped **basil** per quantity

75 g (3 oz) **rocket**

1 ball of **mozzarella cheese**, about 125 g (4 oz)

small bunch of **basil**

salt and **black pepper**

Heat the oil in a frying pan and fry the onion and garlic over a medium heat for 4 minutes or until softened. Set aside to cool.

Place the beef, onion and garlic mixture, herbs, Parmesan, tomatoes and olives in a large bowl, season with salt and pepper and mix well. Divide the mixture into eighths and shape into 8 even-sized patties. Cover and chill for 30 minutes.

Brush the patties with a little oil and cook on a hot barbecue for 4—5 minutes on each side until slightly charred on the outside and medium in the centre.

Meanwhile, toast the halved focaccia quarters on the barbecue for 1 minute on each side until browned.

Spread the base of each bun with some basil mayonnaise and top with some of the rocket and a cooked patty. Tear the mozzarella ball into pieces and divide among the 8 burgers. Top with the lids and a basil leaf and secure with a cocktail stick. Serve with extra basil mayonnaise and rocket, if liked.

For beetroot & horseradish burgers, make and cook the patties as above. Combine 1 tablespoon creamed horseradish with 150 g (5 oz) soured cream and some salt and pepper. Place the patties in 2 large halved rolls with some sliced cooked beetroot, a handful of rocket leaves and a spoonful of the horseradish cream. Cut the rolls into quarters and serve.

thai chicken burgers

Serves **4**

Preparation time **20 minutes,**
plus chilling

Cooking time **14–16 minutes**

500 g (1 lb) skinless **chicken
breast fillets**, minced

1–2 tablespoons **Thai red
curry paste**

1 small **onion**, finely chopped

2 tablespoons chopped
coriander

olive oil, for brushing

4 **oval buns,** halved

50 g (2 oz) mixed **Asian salad
leaves**

handful of mixed **Thai** or **plain
basil, coriander** and **mint
leaves**

Coconut satay sauce

6 tablespoons **coconut cream**

3 tablespoons **smooth
peanut butter**

juice of ½ **lime**

2 teaspoons **Thai fish sauce**

2 teaspoons **sweet chilli
sauce**

Place the chicken, curry paste, onion, coriander and some salt and pepper in a food processor or blender and blend until smooth. Transfer to a bowl and chill for 30 minutes. Divide the mixture into quarters and shape into 8 even-sized patties.

Meanwhile, put all the satay sauce ingredients in a small saucepan and heat gently, stirring until combined. Simmer gently for 1–2 minutes until thickened, then set aside to cool.

Brush the patties lightly with oil and cook on a hot barbecue for 5–6 minutes on each side until cooked though. Test one by inserting a skewer into the centre: it should feel hot to the touch when the burger is cooked.

Fill the buns with the chicken burgers, Asian salad leaves and mixed herbs and spoon the coconut satay sauce over the top.

For quick chicken fillet burgers with sweet chilli sauce, cut 2 large skinless chicken breast fillets in half horizontally to give 4 thinner fillets. Season with salt and pepper, brush with oil and cook on a hot barbecue for 4–5 minutes on each side. Squeeze over the juice of 1 lime and pop into 4 toasted buns with some salad leaves, herbs and sweet chilli sauce.

pork burgers with grilled pears

Serves **4**
Preparation time **5 minutes**
Cooking time **20 minutes**

25 g (1 oz) **butter**
2 **pears**, cut into quarters
6 tablespoons **maple syrup**
1 tablespoon **red wine vinegar**
1 tablespoon **wholegrain mustard**
2 teaspoons peeled and grated **fresh root ginger**
1 tablespoon chopped **sage leaves**
4 **pork loin medallions**, about 125 g (4 oz) each
4 **soft rolls**, halved
salad leaves
salt and **black pepper**

Heat the butter in a frying pan, add the pears and fry until lightly browned. Add 2 tablespoons of the maple syrup and cook until lightly caramelized. Transfer to a roasting dish and baked in a preheated oven, 200°C (400°F), Gas Mark 6, for 10 minutes or until cooked through. Keep warm until needed.

Meanwhile, whisk together the remaining maple syrup with the vinegar, mustard, ginger, sage and a little salt and pepper in a small bowl until they form a sauce.

Place the pork fillets on a hot barbecue and brush with the sauce. Cook for 4—5 minutes on each side, basting with the sauce at regular intervals, until the pork is glossy and cooked through.

Toast the rolls on the barbecue for 1 minute on each side until browned. Fill each one with salad leaves, a pork steak and some of the baked pears.

For maple syrup-glazed pork fillet, combine 1 tablespoon maple syrup with 2 tablespoons olive oil, 1 tablespoon wholegrain mustard, 2 teaspoons ground coriander and some salt and pepper. Brush this over 2 x 400 g (13 oz) pork fillets and leave to marinate for 1 hour. Remove the pork from the marinade, cut in half crossways and cook on a medium-hot barbecue for 10—12 minutes, turning halfway, until cooked. Leave to rest for 5 minutes, then serve in slices with a green salad.

minted lamb kebabs

Serves **4**

Preparation time **15 minutes**, plus chilling

Cooking time **6—8 minutes**

500 g (1 lb) boneless **leg of lamb**, minced

1 small **onion**, finely chopped

1 **garlic clove**, crushed

1 tablespoon chopped **rosemary**

6 **anchovies in oil**, drained and chopped

olive oil, for brushing

salt and **black pepper**

Tomato & olive salad

6 ripe **tomatoes**, cut into wedges

1 **red onion**, sliced

125 g (4 oz) pitted **black olives**

a few torn **basil leaves**

2 tablespoons **extra virgin olive oil**

a squeeze of **lemon juice**

Combine the lamb, onion, garlic, rosemary, anchovies and some salt and pepper in a bowl and use your hands to work them together. Divide into 12 and shape into even-sized, sausage-shaped patties. Chill for 30 minutes.

Thread the patties on to metal skewers, brush lightly with oil and barbecue for 3—4 minutes on each side until cooked through. Keep warm.

Meanwhile, make the salad. Combine the tomatoes, onion, olives and basil in a bowl and season with salt and pepper. Drizzle with oil and squeeze a little lemon juice over. Serve the kebabs with the salad.

For lamb souvlaki, cube 750 g (1½ lb) lamb shoulder and place in a bowl. Add 300 ml (½ pint) red wine, 2 tablespoons red wine vinegar, 1 chopped onion, 2 chopped garlic cloves, 2 tablespoons dried oregano, 1 tablespoon extra virgin olive oil and a little salt and pepper and leave to marinate for at least 4 hours. Remove the meat from the marinade and thread on to skewers. Cook on a hot barbecue for 4—5 minutes on each side and serve with the salad and some tzatziki.

breakfast burger with mushrooms

Serves **4**
Preparation time **15 minutes**,
  plus chilling
Cooking time **10—12 minutes**

750 g (1½ lb) boneless **pork
  shoulder**, minced
2 **garlic cloves**, crushed
1 tablespoon chopped **thyme**
2 tablespoons **cornflour**
1 **egg**, lightly beaten
spray oil
4 large **flat mushrooms**,
  trimmed
4 **back bacon rashers**, rind
  removed
4 large **sesame seed rolls**,
  halved
2 ripe **tomatoes**, sliced
American-style mustard or
  mayonnaise (optional)
salt and **black pepper**
tomato sauce, to serve

Combine the pork, garlic, thyme, cornflour, egg and some salt and pepper in a bowl and, using your hands, work together until well blended. Divide the mixture into quarters and shape into 4 even-sized patties. Chill for 30 minutes.

Spray the patties with a little oil and cook on a hot barbecue for 5—6 minutes on each side. Set aside to rest until required. Barbecue the mushrooms for 2—3 minutes on each side and the bacon for 2 minutes on each side.

Place the patties on the sesame rolls and top with the mushrooms, bacon and tomatoes and some mustard, if liked. Serve with tomato sauce.

For vegetarian breakfast burgers, cook 4 large flat mushrooms as above and keep warm. Cook 2 halved tomatoes for 30 seconds on each side. Fry 4 free-range eggs in a little oil on the flat plate of a gas barbecue or in a frying pan for charcoal. Arrange the mushrooms, grilled tomatoes and fried eggs in 4 wholemeal buns and serve with some baby spinach leaves and a spoonful of Pesto (see page 158).

barbecued pork sandwich

Serves **8**

Preparation time **45 minutes**, plus marinating

Cooking time **1—1¼ hours**

2 tablespoons **Smoky Barbecue Rub** (see page 194)

1 kg (2 lb) **boneless pork shoulder**

8 **bread rolls**

Coleslaw

250 g (8 oz) **white cabbage**, shredded

175 g (6 oz) **carrots**, grated

½ **white onion**, thinly sliced

1 teaspoon **salt**

2 teaspoons **caster sugar**

1 tablespoon **white wine vinegar**

75 g (3 oz) **mayonnaise**

black pepper

Rub the spice rub into the pork and leave to marinate overnight in the refrigerator. Return the pork to room temperature for 1 hour before cooking.

Make the coleslaw when you are ready to cook. Put the cabbage, carrots and onion in a colander and sprinkle with the salt, sugar and vinegar. Stir well, then leave to drain over a bowl for 30 minutes. Squeeze out any excess liquid from the vegetables and place in a large bowl. Mix the mayonnaise into the cabbage mixture and season with pepper to taste. Set aside until required.

Cook the pork by the indirect grilling method (see page 12) on a medium barbecue for 1—1¼ hours until tender. Wrap loosely in foil and set aside to rest for 15 minutes. Finely slice the pork and serve in rolls with the coleslaw.

For barbecued pork chops with grilled apple wedges, season 4 x 250 g (8 oz) pork chops with salt and pepper and cook on a medium-hot barbecue for 4—5 minutes on each side. Wrap in foil and set aside to rest for 3 minutes. Meanwhile, cut 2 cored apples into large wedges, spray with oil and grill for 1 minute on each side until golden and cooked. Serve the chops with the grilled apples and a green salad.

pancetta hot dogs with salsa rossa

Serves **4**
Preparation time **15 minutes**
Cooking time **35 minutes**

6 slices of **smoked pancetta**
12 small **Italian sausages** or
  chipolatas
1 large **onion**, cut into 8 thick
  wedges
12 large **bay leaves**

Salsa rossa
1 large **red pepper**
1 tablespoon **extra virgin
  olive oil**
2 **garlic cloves**, crushed
2 large ripe **tomatoes**, peeled
  and roughly chopped
½ teaspoon **cayenne pepper**
1 tablespoon **red wine
  vinegar**
salt and **black pepper**

Start by making the salsa rossa. Cook the pepper on a
hot barbecue until charred all over, then put in a plastic
bag, seal and leave to cool. When cool, peel and
discard the seeds, reserving any juices, and chop
the flesh.

Heat the oil in a pan, sauté the garlic for 3 minutes,
then add the tomatoes and cayenne pepper and
simmer gently for 15 minutes. Stir in the peppers and
the vinegar, season with salt and pepper and simmer
for a further 5 minutes to cook off the excess liquid.
Purée in a food processor or blender until smooth,
then set aside.

Cut the pancetta slices in half crossways and wrap
each half around 1 sausage. Thread on to 4 large
metal skewers, alternating with the wedges of onion
and bay leaves, so that each skewer has 3 sausages,
2 onion wedges and 3 bay leaves. Cook on a hot
barbecue for 5 minutes until charred and cooked
through. Serve with the salsa rossa, reheated if
necessary.

For chargrilled chicken & salsa rossa sandwiches,
cut 2 chicken breast fillets in half crossways to give
4 thin fillets and season well. Cook on a hot barbecue
for 4–5 minutes on each side, then set aside to rest
for 3 minutes. Lightly toast 4 burger rolls and fill each
with a chicken fillet, some salsa rossa and 25 g (1 oz)
rocket leaves for each roll.

shish kebabs

Serves **6**
Preparation time **15 minutes**,
  plus marinating
Cooking time **10–15 minutes**

375 g (12 oz) **minced lamb**
1 **onion**, finely chopped
2 teaspoons **lemon juice**
1 **egg**, beaten
2 tablespoons **plain flour**
2 tablespoons chopped
  coriander
½ teaspoon **salt**
oil, for brushing

Marinade
4 tablespoons **natural yogurt**
1 tablespoon **medium** or **hot
  curry powder**
1 **garlic clove**, crushed

To garnish
red onion, finely sliced
red pepper, finely sliced
1 tablespoon chopped
  parsley
1 teaspoon **paprika**
lime wedges

Mix all the ingredients except for the oil in a large bowl until smooth. Divide the mixture into 6 and form into even-sized, sausage-shaped patties.

Make the marinade. Mix the yogurt, curry powder and garlic in a flat-based dish. Thread the patties on to oiled metal skewers and leave to marinate for 2–4 hours.

Remove the skewers from the marinade. Brush the patties with oil and cook on a medium-hot barbecue for 10–15 minutes, turning occasionally.

Serve hot, garnished with the onion, pepper and parsley, dusted over with paprika, and with lime wedges to squeeze over.

For shish kebab pittas, make and cook the patties as above, then stuff into 6 warmed pitta breads with shredded lettuce, sliced tomatoes and some Tahini Sauce (see page 98).

monkfish & prawn kebabs

Serves **4**
Preparation time **15 minutes**,
   plus soaking and marinating
Cooking time **4–6 minutes**

8 large **rosemary sprigs**
500 g (1 lb) **monkfish fillets**,
   cut into 16 large chunks
16 raw peeled **tiger prawns**,
   deveined
2 **garlic cloves**, crushed
grated rind and juice of
   1 **lemon**
1½ tablespoons **extra virgin**
   olive oil
1 recipe quantity **Aïoli**
   (see page 122) with
   1 tablespoon **lemon juice**
   added with the egg yolks

Rip the rosemary leaves from the stalks, leaving a few rosemary leaves on the end of each sprig. Cut the other end on a diagonal to form a sharp tip. Soak in cold water for 30 minutes. Finely chop 1 tablespoon of the rosemary leaves, reserving the rest for another dish.

Thread the fish chunks on to the soaked rosemary skewers, alternating with the prawns, allowing 2 cubes of fish and 2 prawns per skewer. Place in a shallow nonmetallic dish.

Combine the chopped rosemary, garlic, lemon rind and some salt and black pepper with the oil, pour over the kebabs and leave to marinate for 1 hour. Remove from the marinade. Cook on a hot barbecue for 2–3 minutes on each side until cooked, squeeze the lemon juice over the kebabs and serve with the lemon aïoli.

For grilled monkfish wrapped in Parma ham, wrap 4 x 200 g (7 oz) monkfish fillets in a large slice of Parma ham each and secure with cocktail sticks. Brush with oil and cook on a hot barbecue for 5–6 minutes, turning halfway through. Leave to rest for 5 minutes, then serve with aïoli and a rocket salad.

swordfish kebabs with tahini sauce

Serves **4**

Preparation time **20 minutes**, plus marinating

Cooking time **4—6 minutes**

1 kg (2 lb) **swordfish steaks**, cubed

2 teaspoons **ground turmeric**

1 teaspoon **ground cinnamon**

grated rind of 1 **lemon**

2 tablespoons **extra virgin olive oil**

8 x 23 cm (9 inch) **flour tortillas**

100 g (3½ oz) **salad leaves**

4 ripe **tomatoes**, cut into wedges

a few **mint leaves**, torn

salt and **black pepper**

Tahini sauce

150 g (5 oz) **Greek-style yogurt**

2 teaspoons **tahini**

1 teaspoon **lemon juice**

1 small **garlic clove**, crushed

Soak 8 double prong bamboo skewers in cold water for 30 minutes (you can use normal bamboo skewers, if preferred). Place the swordfish in a shallow bowl, rub in the turmeric, cinnamon, lemon rind, oil and some salt and pepper and leave to marinate for 15 minutes. Thread on to the skewers and cook over hot coals for 2—3 minutes on each side.

Meanwhile, place the tahini sauce ingredients in a bowl and stir well until combined. Season to taste with salt and pepper.

Arrange half the flour tortillas on plates and top with salad leaves, tomatoes, mint, the fish skewers and some tahini sauce. Wrap and push to one side. Repeat with the remaining tortillas and filling ingredients, then serve.

For grilled swordfish sandwiches, season 4 x 200 g (7 oz) swordfish steaks with salt and pepper and barbecue for 1—1½ minutes on each side. Meanwhile, lightly toast 8 slices of sourdough bread. Cover half the slices with the swordfish steaks, rocket and some Pesto (see page 158), then add the sandwich tops and serve.

prawn kebabs

Serves **4**
Preparation time **10 minutes**,
  plus marinating
Cooking time **18—23 minutes**

12 **Dublin Bay prawns**,
  thawed if frozen, peeled with
  tails left on, deveined
175 g (6 oz) **long-grain rice**
175 g (6 oz) frozen **peas**
8 **streaky bacon rashers**, rind
  removed, halved lengthways
  and rolled up
50 g (2 oz) **margarine** or
  butter
125 g (4 oz) **mushrooms**,
  trimmed and sliced

Balsamic marinade
5 tablespoons **olive oil**
2 tablespoons **balsamic
  vinegar**
2 tablespoons chopped
  oregano or **marjoram**
2 **garlic cloves**, crushed
black pepper

Mix all the marinade ingredients in a shallow bowl. Add the prawns to the marinade, turning to coat thoroughly. Cover and leave to marinate for 1 hour.

Put the rice in a large saucepan of boiling salted water and cook for 12—15 minutes or until just tender. Pour into a colander to drain.

Meanwhile, cook the peas in a separate saucepan of simmering salted water for about 5 minutes or until they are just tender. Drain the peas thoroughly.

Drain the prawns, reserving the marinade, and thread on to 4 metal skewers, alternating with the bacon rolls.

Cook on a hot barbecue for 6—8 minutes, turning the skewers several times and brushing the prawns and bacon with the remaining marinade, until the prawns are tender and cooked through and the bacon is crisp.

Meanwhile, melt the margarine in a saucepan, add the mushrooms and fry gently for about 3 minutes, until soft.

Stir the rice and peas into the pan and season to taste. Pile the rice mixture on to a heated serving dish and serve with the kebabs arranged on top.

For minted seafood kebabs, marinate 250 g (8 oz) each of cubed monkfish and salmon in lime yogurt marinade (see page 186) for 30 minutes. Remove from the marinade and thread alternately on to soaked bamboo skewers. Cook on a medium-hot barbecue for 3—4 minutes on each side until cooked through. Serve with the vegetable rice as above.

chicken satay sticks

Serves **4**
Preparation time **10 minutes**,
  plus marinating
Cooking time **4–6 minutes**

4 skinless **chicken fillets**,
  about 125 g (4 oz) each,
  sliced lengthways into
  3 strips
chopped **coriander**, to garnish

Marinade
4 tablespoons **soy sauce**
4 tablespoons **lime juice**
1 **garlic clove**, crushed
1 teaspoon **curry powder**
1 teaspoon **peanut butter**
pinch of **dried chilli flakes**

Satay sauce
1 tablespoon **peanut butter**
2 tablespoons **lime juice**
1 teaspoon **curry powder**
1 **garlic clove**, crushed
4 tablespoons **water**

Soak 12 bamboo skewers in cold water for 30 minutes. Put all the marinade ingredients in a shallow dish and mix until smooth.

Thread the pieces of chicken on to the skewers. Place in the dish of marinade, coat well and leave to marinate at room temperature for up to 2 hours.

Put all the sauce ingredients in a small bowl and mix until smooth.

Cook the chicken sticks on a hot barbecue for 2–3 minutes on each side. Garnish with chopped coriander and serve with plenty of the satay sauce for dipping.

For beef satay sticks, cut 500 g (1 lb) beef fillet into thin strips and thread on to 12 soaked skewers, zig-zagging back and forth as you go. Marinate in the satay sauce as above, then cook on a hot barbecue for 2–3 minutes on each side. Serve with Nam Jim Dressing (see page 112)

seafood

moroccan salmon with fattoush

Serves **4**
Preparation time **20 minutes**,
  plus marinating
Cooking time **7–9 minutes**

4 **salmon fillets**, about 200 g
  (7 oz) each
1 quantity **Moroccan Spice
  Paste** (see page 190)
spray oil

Fattoush salad
1 **green pepper**, deseeded
  and diced
1 **Lebanese cucumber**, diced
2 ripe **tomatoes**, diced
½ **red onion**, finely chopped
2 tablespoons chopped
  parsley
2 tablespoons chopped
  coriander
2 large **flatbreads**
3 tablespoons **extra virgin
  olive oil**
1 tablespoon **lemon juice**
salt and **black pepper**

Use tweezers to remove any small bones from the
salmon fillets and place in a ceramic fish. Add the
spice paste and rub all over the fish. Marinate for
2–4 hours.

Make the salad. Mix together the pepper, cucumber,
tomatoes and onion and herbs in a bowl. Toast the
flatbreads on a hot barbecue for 30 seconds or so on
each side, cool slightly and tear into bite-sized pieces.
Add to the bowl with the olive oil and lemon juice.
Season and stir well.

Remove the fish from its dish, spray with a little oil
and cook on the hot barbecue for 3–4 minutes on
each side until lightly charred and cooked to your
liking. Rest briefly, then serve with the salad.

For salmon wrapped in prosciutto, wrap 4 x 200 g
(7 oz) skinless salmon fillets in a slice of prosciutto,
securing in place with a cocktail stick. Cook the
parcels on a hot barbecue for 3–4 minutes on
each side, rest briefly and serve with Salsa Rossa
(see page 92).

red mullet & vine leaf parcels

Serves **4**
Preparation time **20 minutes**
Cooking time **8–10 minutes**

6 tablespoons **olive oil**
2 tablespoons **lemon juice**
2 tablespoons chopped **dill**
2 **spring onions**, chopped
1 teaspoon **mustard powder**
8 **vine leaves** in brine, drained
4 **red mullet**, about 350 g
   (12 oz) each, scaled and
   gutted
4 **bay leaves**
4 **dill sprigs**, plus extra to
   garnish
salt and **black pepper**
lemon wedges, to garnish

Put 4 pieces of string, about 30 cm (12 inches) long, into cold water to soak for 10 minutes.

Put the oil, lemon juice, chopped dill, spring onions, mustard powder and salt and pepper in a bowl and mix well. Wash and dry the vine leaves and arrange them in pairs, overlapping them slightly.

Make several slashes on both sides of each fish and rub them all over with a little of the oil and lemon mixture. Stuff each of the belly cavities with a bay leaf and a dill sprig. Lay each fish on a pair of vine leaves and wrap securely. Brush with a little of the oil and lemon mixture and fasten with the wet string to secure the leaves in place.

Cook the fish on a hot barbecue for 4–5 minutes on each side, brushing them with a little more of the oil and lemon mixture if necessary, until lightly charred. Leave the fish to rest for a few minutes, then discard the string and vine leaves and dress the mullet with the rest of the oil and lemon mixture. Garnish with dill sprigs and serve with a Tomato & Olive Salad (see page 86), if liked.

For goats' cheese & vine leaf parcels, cut 250 g (8 oz) goats' cheese log into 8 thick slices. Place a slice in the middle of a large washed and dried vine leaf, wrap the leaf over and around the cheese slice and secure with cooking string. Repeat to make 8 parcels. Cook on a hot barbecue for 2–3 minutes on each side until the cheese starts to ooze. Serve spread on slices of toasted French bread.

clam parcels with coconut

Serves **4**
Preparation time **10 minutes**,
  plus soaking
Cooking time **8 minutes**

2 kg (4 lb) **fresh clams**
2 **garlic cloves**, chopped
2 teaspoons peeled and
  grated **fresh root ginger**
1 large **red chilli**, deseeded
  and finely chopped
8 **lime leaves**, torn
1 **lemon grass stalk**, bruised
  and roughly chopped
200 ml (7 fl oz) carton
  coconut cream
juice of 1 **lime**
1 tablespoon **light brown
  soft sugar**
chopped **coriander**, to garnish
crusty **bread**, to serve

Soak the clams in plenty of cold water for 1 hour, then drain, wash the clams and scrub the shells if they appear dirty. Arrange 4 large pieces of foil on a work surface and place a quarter of the clams in the centre of each one. Top each one with a quarter of the garlic, ginger, chilli, lime leaves and lemon grass and draw the edges of the foil up to form 'cups'.

Combine the coconut cream, lime juice and sugar and pour a quarter into each 'cup'. Seal the edges of the foil and cook the parcels on a hot barbecue for 8 minutes. Transfer the parcels to 4 plates, garnish with coriander and serve with crusty bread.

For clam parcels with garlic & chive butter, beat together 125 g (4 oz) softened butter, 1 crushed garlic clove, 2 tablespoons snipped chives and some black pepper. Divide the clams between foil 'cups', following the method above, and add 2 tablespoons dry white wine to each one. Dot with the flavoured butter, then seal the parcels. Cook as above and serve with crusty bread.

scallops with nam jim dressing

Serves **4**
Preparation time **5 minutes**
Cooking time **3 minutes**

24 **scallops on the half shell**
or **shelled**

Nam jim dressing
1 large **red chilli**, deseeded
and roughly chopped
1 **red birds eye chilli**,
deseeded and roughly
chopped
2 **garlic cloves**, chopped
pinch of **salt**
1 tablespoon chopped
coriander
25 g (1 oz) **palm sugar**, grated
or **dark soft brown sugar**
1 tablespoon **Thai fish sauce**
2 tablespoons freshly
squeezed **lime juice**

Start by making the dressing. Pound the chillies, garlic
and salt to form a rough paste using a pestle and
mortar. Transfer to a bowl and stir in the coriander,
palm sugar, fish sauce and lime juice, then stir until
the sugar has dissolved.

Loosen the scallops from their shells with a small
knife. Place the shells on a hot barbecue and cook for
3 minutes. Arrange the shells on plates and top each
one with a spoonful of the dressing. Serve hot.

Alternatively, thread shelled scallops on to bamboo
skewers that have been soaked in cold water for 30
minutes. Cook for 1 minute on each side and serve
with the dressing.

For scallops with preserved lemon salsa, combine
25 g (1 oz) diced preserved lemon, 25 g (1 oz) diced
semi-dried tomatoes, 2 finely chopped spring onions,
1 tablespoon chopped basil, 4 tablespoons extra
virgin olive oil and some salt and pepper. Cook the
scallops following the above method and serve
topped with the preserved lemon salsa.

chargrilled squid with chilli jam

Serves **4**
Preparation time **15 minutes**,
    plus cooling and marinating
Cooking time **50 minutes**

1 kg (2 lb) cleaned **squid**
2–4 **garlic cloves**, crushed
1 tablespoon **sea salt**
1 tablespoon **light brown
    soft sugar**
lime wedges, to garnish

Chilli jam
4 **birds eye chillies**
500 g (1 lb) **tomatoes**
2 **garlic cloves**, crushed
175 g (6 oz) **light brown
    soft sugar**
125 ml (4 fl oz) **red wine
    vinegar**
salt and **black pepper**

Place all the chilli jam ingredients in a saucepan, bring the mixture to the boil and simmer for 45 minutes until thickened and jam-like. Leave to cool completely.

Remove the tentacles from inside the squid bodies and slice the tentacles away from the beak part of the head. Remove the quill from inside each body, if present.

Cut the bodies in half lengthways and then again crossways, then, using a sharp knife, score the inside with a diamond pattern. Place the squid pieces in a bowl. Add the garlic, salt and sugar and rub in well, then leave to marinate for 15 minutes.

Cook the squid on a hot barbecue for 1–2 minutes, garnish with lime wedges and serve with the chilli jam.

For squid piri-piri, make some Piri-piri Sauce (see page 198). Take 8 medium-sized squid bodies and cut in half lengthways. Score the bodies as above, brush with oil and season with salt and pepper. Cook on a hot barbecue for 1–2 minutes, then transfer to a board and cut into small pieces. Serve with the piri-piri sauce drizzled over.

prawns with asian dressing

Serves **4**

Preparation time **10 minutes**, plus marinating

Cooking time **6 minutes**

24 raw peeled large **prawns**, deveined

Marinade

4 tablespoons **olive oil**

2 **garlic cloves**, sliced

2 teaspoons peeled and grated **fresh root ginger**

1 **red birds eye chilli**, deseeded and sliced

4 **lime leaves**, torn

1 **lemon grass stalk**, finely sliced

2 tablespoons **Thai fish sauce**

2 tablespoons **lime juice**

4 teaspoons **light brown soft sugar**

salt and **black pepper**

To garnish

1 tablespoon each chopped **coriander, mint** and **Thai basil leaves**

1 large **red chilli**, deseeded and sliced

Combine the marinade ingredients in a nonmetallic dish. Add the prawns and stir well, then leave to marinate for 30 minutes. Meanwhile, soak 24 bamboo skewers in cold water for 30 minutes.

Thread one prawn on to each skewer and tip the marinade juices into a small pan.

Cook the prawns on a hot barbecue for 2 minutes on each side, then arrange on a platter. Heat the pan juices until they come to the boil, then pour over the prawns. Serve garnished with the herbs and chilli slices.

For Asian mixed-leaf salad, to serve as an accompaniment, place 125 g (4 oz) mixed Asian leaves in a bowl. Add 1 finely grated carrot, ½ deseeded and finely sliced cucumber and 50 g (2 oz) bean sprouts. Whisk 2 tablespoons extra virgin olive oil with 2 teaspoons light soy sauce, 1 teaspoon lime juice and 1 teaspoon clear honey, add the dressing to the salad and toss well.

sea bass with lime aïoli

Serves **4**
Preparation time **30 minutes**
Cooking time **20–25 minutes**

4 large **potatoes**, scrubbed
4 tablespoons **olive oil**
4 **sea bass fillets**, 175–250 g
  (6–8 oz) each
salt and **black pepper**

Lime aïoli
4–6 **garlic cloves**, crushed
2 **egg yolks**
juice and finely grated rind of
  2 **limes**
300 ml (½ pint) **extra virgin
  olive oil**

To garnish
grilled **lime slices**
snipped **chives**

Make the aïoli by placing the garlic and egg yolks in a food processor or blender, adding the lime juice and processing briefly to mix. With the machine running, gradually add the olive oil in a thin, steady stream until the mixture forms a thick cream. Turn into a bowl, stir in the lime rind, and season with salt and pepper. Set aside.

Slice the potatoes thinly and brush well with olive oil. Sprinkle the slices with salt and pepper and cook on a hot barbecue for 8–10 minutes on each side or until tender and golden. Remove from the heat and keep warm.

Score the sea bass fillets, brush well with the remaining olive oil and cook, skin side down, on the barbecue for 3–4 minutes until just cooked, turning once. Remove from the heat and serve the fish, potatoes and aïoli garnished with lime slices and snipped chives.

For soy & ginger sea bass parcels, place 4 x 200 g (7 oz) sea bass fillets in the centre of 4 large squares of foil. Top each with a little sliced spring onion, some shredded ginger, a slice of garlic and a star anise. Combine 1 tablespoon dark soy sauce with the juice of ½ lime, 2 tablespoons rice wine (or dry sherry) and 2 teaspoons sesame oil and divide between the fish portions. Wrap up to form parcels and cook on a hot barbecue for 5 minutes. Remove and leave to rest for 5 minutes, then serve with steamed rice.

blackened tuna with mango salsa

Serves **4**
Preparation time **10 minutes**,
  plus marinating
Cooking time **2 minutes**

4 **tuna steaks**, about 250 g
  (8 oz) each
1 tablespoon **extra virgin
olive oil**
2 tablespoons freshly crushed
  black pepper
1 teaspoon **salt**
lime slices, to garnish

Mango salsa
1 large **mango**, about 500 g
  (1 lb), diced
½ **red onion**, finely chopped
1 large **red chilli**, deseeded
  and finely chopped
1 tablespoon **lime juice**
2 tablespoons chopped
  coriander
salt and **black pepper**

Make the mango salsa by combining all the ingredients in a bowl and seasoning to taste. Set aside for the flavours to develop.

Brush the tuna steaks with a little oil and season with the peppercorns and salt. Cook the tuna on a hot barbecue for about 1 minute on each side (or a little less if wished). Rest briefly, then serve with the salsa and the lime slices to garnish.

For open-grilled tuna burger, chargrill 4 seasoned tuna steaks, about 250 g (8 oz) each, following the method above, drizzle with lemon juice and leave to rest briefly. Toast 4 bread slices on the barbecue for 1 minute on each side until charred. Remove, then rub with peeled garlic and drizzle with extra virgin olive oil. Top each toast with a tuna steak and the juices and serve topped with rocket leaves, sliced tomatoes and some Aïoli (see page 122).

salt-rubbed prawns with aïoli

Serves **4**
Preparation time **10 minutes**
Cooking time **4–6 minutes**

24 raw **king prawns**
2 tablespoons **extra virgin olive oil**
2 tablespoons **sea salt**

Aïoli
3 **egg yolks**
2 teaspoons **white wine vinegar**
1 teaspoon **Dijon mustard**
2–4 **garlic cloves**, crushed
300 ml (½ pint) **olive oil**
salt and **white pepper**

Place the prawns in a large bowl, add the oil and salt and toss well together so the prawns are lightly coated with the salt.

Make the aïoli. Place the egg yolks, vinegar, mustard, garlic cloves and a little salt and pepper in a food processor and blend briefly until the egg mixture is frothy. Then, with the blade running, gradually pour in the oil through the funnel until the sauce is thickened and glossy. Thin with a little boiling water if the sauce is too thick. Adjust the seasoning to taste.

Cook the prawns on a hot barbecue for 2–3 minutes on each side. Serve with the aïoli to dip the prawns into once they've been peeled, and a rocket salad.

For chargrilled prawns with chilli & garlic butter, peel and devein 24 large prawns and thread on to pre-soaked bamboo skewers. Spray with a little oil and barbecue on a high heat for 3–4 minutes until evenly charred and cooked through. Squeeze over a little lemon juice. Meanwhile, place 1 deseeded and chopped large red chilli, 2 crushed garlic cloves and 125 g (4 oz) butter in a saucepan and heat gently until melted and the garlic is softened, about 3 minutes. Serve the butter as a sauce for the prawns.

swordfish with walnuts & beans

Serves **4**
Preparation time **15 minutes**
Cooking time **6 minutes**

4 **swordfish steaks**, about
   200 g (7 oz) each
extra virgin olive oil, for
   brushing
2 tablespoons **balsamic glaze**
salt and **black pepper**

Salad
250 g (8 oz) **fine green
   beans**, trimmed
250 g (8 oz) **yellow beans**,
   trimmed
50 g (2 oz) **walnuts**, toasted
2 tablespoons torn **parsley
   leaves**
2 tablespoons torn **mint
   leaves**

Dressing
3 tablespoons **walnut oil**
1 tablespoon **extra virgin
   olive oil**
1 tablespoon **sherry vinegar**
1 teaspoon **caster sugar**
1 small **garlic clove**, crushed

Rub the swordfish steaks with oil and season with salt
and pepper.

Make the salad. Cook the beans in a saucepan of
lightly salted boiling water for 3 minutes, drain well and
refresh under cold water. Pat dry. Place in a bowl and
add the walnuts and herbs and a little salt and pepper.

Whisk the dressing ingredients together in a bowl
and season with salt and pepper. Drizzle over the
salad and toss well.

Cook the swordfish steaks on a hot barbecue for
1–1½ minutes on each side. Wrap loosely in foil and
set aside to rest for 3 minutes. Arrange the swordfish
on plates, drizzle with the balsamic glaze and serve
with the bean salad.

For homemade balsamic glaze, pour 500 ml
(15 fl oz) cheap balsamic vinegar into a saucepan
and bring to the boil. Simmer fast for 10–15 minutes
until the vinegar is reduced to about 125 ml (4 fl oz).
Set aside to cool. Store in a clean bottle and use
as required.

buttery lobster tails with aïoli

Serves **4**
Preparation time **20 minutes**
Cooking time **14–16 minutes**

4 raw **lobster tails**
50 g (2 oz) **butter**
2 tablespoons **ready-made**
  or **homemade garlic &**
  saffron oil (see below)
1 tablespoon snipped **chives**
½ recipe quantity **Aïoli**
  (see page 122), with
  ½ tablespoon **lemon juice**
  added with the eggs
cucumber ribbons, made
  using a vegetable peeler

To garnish
finely grated rind of **1 lemon**
2 tablespoons chopped
  chervil

Dot the lobster tails with the butter and drizzle with the garlic and saffron oil. Cook the lobster tails on a hot barbecue for 7–8 minutes each side, or until cooked through.

Stir the chives into the aïoli. Sprinkle the lobster with the lemon rind and chopped chervil and serve immediately with the cucumber ribbons and aïoli in small bowls.

For homemade garlic & saffron oil, which is also perfect for making quick and interesting Italian bruschettas, heat 500 ml (17 fl oz) extra virgin olive oil very gently in a saucepan with 10–12 garlic cloves and 1 teaspoon saffron threads. (The idea is just to warm the oil, not to get it hot.) Remove the pan from the heat and let it cool completely, then pour the oil and the flavourings into a clean bottle and stopper tightly. Leave in a cool place for 2 weeks, then either use immediately or strain to prevent harmful bacteria from growing in it, then pour into a clean bottle and keep for up to 6 months.

olive & citrus salmon

Serves **4**
Preparation time **5 minutes**
Cooking time **8–10 minutes**

4 **salmon fillets**, about 200 g
(7 oz) each
12 large **black olives**, pitted
and halved
12 **cherry tomatoes**, halved
4 tablespoons **extra virgin
olive oil**
2 wedges **preserved lemon**,
thinly sliced
2 teaspoons **clear honey**
salt and **black pepper**
chopped **parsley**, to garnish

Use tweezers to remove any small bones from the salmon fillets. Place on 4 large pieces of foil and top each with a quarter of the olives, tomatoes, oil, preserved lemon and honey. Season with salt and pepper and seal the parcels well.

Cook the parcels on a hot barbecue for 8–10 minutes, then remove from the heat and rest briefly. Carefully open the parcels, garnish with chopped parsley and serve with a Couscous Salad (see page 156).

For foil-wrapped cod with soy, ginger & sesame, place 4 cod fillets on foil, as above, drawing the edges up slightly to form 'cups'. Add 1 tablespoon dry sherry, 1 tablespoon dark soy sauce, a little shredded fresh root ginger, a little sliced garlic and 1 teaspoon sesame oil to each one. Seal the foil and cook as above. Serve with plain boiled rice.

juniper & peppercorn salmon

Serves **6**

Preparation time **10 minutes**, plus marinating

Cooking time **8–10 minutes**

6 **salmon fillets**, about 200 g (7 oz) each

frisée lettuce leaves, to serve

Juniper & peppercorn marinade

1½ tablespoons **dried juniper berries**

2 teaspoons **dried green peppercorns**

¼ teaspoon **black peppercorns**

1 teaspoon **demerara sugar**

2–3 tablespoons **oil**

To garnish

lemon wedges

parsley sprigs

2 **spring onions**, finely shredded

Make the marinade by coarsely grinding the juniper berries and peppercorns in a spice grinder or using a pestle and mortar. Mix with the sugar and oil.

Use tweezers to remove any small bones from the salmon fillets. Brush the fillets with the marinade and leave to marinate at room temperature for 1 hour.

Wrap each salmon fillet in a piece of foil, sealing the edges well. Cook on a hot barbecue for 8–10 minutes, then set aside to rest briefly. Unwrap the salmon, garnish with lemon wedges, parsley sprigs and spring onions and serve with frisée lettuce leaves.

For pork fillet with juniper & peppercorns, make the marinade as above and place in a shallow dish. Trim 4 x 200 g (7 oz) pork tenderloins and coat with the marinade. Cover and chill for 2 hours. Remove the pork and cook on a medium-hot barbecue for 12–15 minutes until evenly browned. Leave to rest for 5 minutes, then serve with Spinach Salad (see page 60).

mackerel with citrus fennel salad

Serves **4**

Preparation time **10 minutes**

Cooking time **8–10 minutes**

4 **mackerel**, about 400 g
   (13 oz) each

spray oil

3 **lemons**, thinly sliced, plus
   2 tablespoons lemon juice

1 **fennel bulb**, trimmed and
   thinly sliced, fronds reserved

1 small **garlic clove**, crushed

2 tablespoons drained **capers**

2 tablespoons **extra virgin
   olive oil**

1 tablespoon chopped
   parsley

salt and **black pepper**

Slash each mackerel 3–4 times on each side with a sharp knife. Spray with a little oil and season inside and out with salt and pepper. Using cooking string, tie 3 lemon slices on each side of the fish. Spray with a little oil and cook on a hot barbecue for 4–5 minutes on each side until lightly charred and cooked through. Set aside to rest for 5 minutes.

Place the fennel in a bowl with the garlic, capers, oil, parsley, fennel fronds and lemon juice and season to taste. Serve the mackerel with the fennel salad.

For chargrilled sardines with salsa verde, prepare 20 medium sardines following the method above and cook on a hot barbecue for 3–4 minutes on each side. Squeeze with lemon juice and serve the sardines with Salsa Verde (see page 48).

vegetarian
dishes

sweetcorn with chilli salt

Serves **6**
Preparation time **5 minutes**
Cooking time **25 minutes**

6 **sweetcorn cobs**, husked
   and trimmed
2 tablespoons **sea salt**
½ teaspoon **dried red chilli
   flakes**
65 g (2½ oz) **butter**
1 **lime**, cut into wedges,
   to garnish

Blanch the corn in a large saucepan in 2 separate batches for 10 minutes. Drain well and pat dry on kitchen paper. Cook the cobs on a hot barbecue for 5–6 minutes, turning frequently, until evenly charred and tender.

Meanwhile, place the salt and chilli flakes in a mortar and pound with a pestle until the salt turns a rusty red.

Place the corn on plates and top with butter, sprinkle with the chilli salt and garnish with the lime wedges.

For smoky sweetcorn salsa, follow the recipe above to cook and barbecue 1 sweetcorn cob, then, using a sharp knife, cut down the cob to remove the kernels. Place in a bowl and, when cool, stir in 2 finely chopped spring onions, 1 deseeded and chopped tomato, 1 deseeded and finely chopped large red chilli, 1 crushed garlic clove, juice of ½ lime, 2 tablespoons chopped coriander and some salt and pepper.

mustard & thyme sweet potatoes

Serves **6**
Preparation time **5 minutes**
Cooking time **40 minutes**

6 **sweet potatoes**, about
   250 g (8 oz) each, scrubbed

Mustard & thyme butter
125 g (4 oz) **butter**, softened
1 tablespoon **wholegrain
   mustard**
1 teaspoon chopped **thyme**
black pepper

Wrap each potato in a double layer of foil and either place them on the flat plate of a gas barbecue or, using barbecue tongs, set them in among the heated coals of a charcoal barbecue, allowing some of the coals to cover the potatoes. Bake for 40 minutes.

Meanwhile, make the butter. Place the butter, mustard, thyme and some pepper in a bowl and mash with a fork until evenly mixed. Set aside.

Remove the potatoes from the barbecue (again using tongs) and carefully remove the foil using oven gloves. Cut the potatoes in half and serve topped with the butter.

For classic sweet potato wedges, cut 4 small sweet potatoes into wedges and brush with a little oil. Season with salt and pepper and cook over a medium heat for 30 minutes, turning halfway through until charred and cooked through. Scatter with some sea salt to serve.

spinach & sweet potato cakes

Serves **4**
Preparation time **35 minutes**,
  plus infusing
Cooking time **40 minutes**

500 g (1 lb) **sweet potatoes**,
  cut into chunks
125 g (4 oz) **spinach leaves**
4–5 **spring onions**, sliced
125 g (4 oz) **mangetout**,
  finely shredded
75 g (3 oz) **sweetcorn**
50 g (2 oz) pitted **black
  olives**, finely chopped
3 tablespoons **sesame seeds**
4 tablespoons **flour**
olive oil, for brushing
salt and **black pepper**

Chilli & coconut dip
200 ml (7 fl oz) **coconut cream**
2 **red chillies**, deseeded and
  finely chopped
1 **lemon grass stalk**, sliced
3 **kaffir lime leaves**, shredded
bunch of **coriander**, chopped
1 tablespoon **light soy sauce**
2 tablespoons **sesame oil**

To garnish
lime wedges
spring onions, shredded

Bring a large saucepan of salted water to the boil, add the sweet potatoes and cook for about 20 minutes until tender. Drain the potatoes, then return them to the pan and place over a low heat for 1 minute, stirring constantly to evaporate any excess moisture. Lightly mash the potatoes with a fork.

Meanwhile, put the spinach leaves in a colander and pour a pan of boiling water over. Rinse the spinach with cold water and squeeze the leaves dry. Stir the wilted spinach into the potatoes, then add the spring onions, mangetout, sweetcorn and olives. Season well with salt and pepper and set aside to cool.

Make the dip. Gently warm the coconut cream in a small saucepan with the chillies, lemon grass and lime leaves for about 10 minutes, without letting it reach boiling point. Set aside to infuse.

Use your hands to form the potato mixture into 12 little cakes. Mix the sesame seeds and flour together and sprinkle the mixture over the cakes. Brush the cakes with a little oil, then cook on a moderately hot barbecue for 4–5 minutes. Once a crisp crust has formed, turn them over and cook for a further 4–5 minutes on the other side.

Stir the coriander, soy sauce and sesame oil into the dip and pour it into individual dishes. Serve immediately with the potato cakes, garnished with lime wedges and shredded spring onions.

bruschetta with charred fennel

Serves **4**
Preparation time **10 minutes**
Cooking time **17 minutes**

2 large **fennel bulbs**, about
  400 g (13 oz) total weight,
  trimmed and fronds reserved
3 tablespoons **extra virgin**
  olive oil
100 g (3½ oz) **feta cheese**,
  diced
100 g (3½ oz) pitted **black**
  olives, halved
2 tablespoons chopped
  parsley
squeeze of **lemon juice**
4 slices of **sourdough bread**
2 **garlic cloves**
50 g (2 oz) **wild rocket**
  leaves
salt and **black pepper**

Cut the fennel bulbs lengthways into 5 mm (¼ inch) thick slices and place in a large bowl. Add 1 tablespoon of the oil and toss well. Cook on a hot barbecue for 15 minutes, turning halfway through, until charred and tender.

Transfer the fennel to a bowl and add the feta, olives, parsley, lemon juice and some salt and pepper and toss well.

Toast the bread slices on the barbecue for 1 minute on each side until browned. Rub the charred bread on both sides with the garlic cloves and drizzle with a little of the remaining oil. Top with the fennel salad and rocket and serve drizzled with the remaining oil.

For bruschetta with grilled peppers, cut 2 large red peppers into quarters and discard the seeds. Brush with a little oil and chargrill for 2–3 minutes on each side until tender. Cool in a plastic bag, then peel and discard the skin and cut the flesh into slices. Combine the peppers with 2 tablespoons extra virgin olive oil, 2 teaspoons balsamic vinegar, 1 crushed garlic clove, 6 quartered cherry tomatoes, a few torn basil leaves and some salt and pepper. Chargrill 4 ciabatta slices following the above recipe and serve topped with the pepper mixture.

tomato, pesto & olive pizza

Serves **2**
Preparation time **15 minutes,**
plus rising
Cooking time **20–24 minutes**

spray oil
2 tablespoons **Pesto** (see
page 158)
200 g (7 oz) **cherry
tomatoes,** halved
150 g (5 oz) **mozzarella
cheese,** sliced
50 g (2 oz) pitted **black
olives,** halved
handful of **basil leaves**
salt and **black pepper**

Pizza dough
250 g (8 oz) **strong white
flour**
½ teaspoon **salt**
1 teaspoon **fast action dried
yeast**
125 ml (4 fl oz) warm **water**
1 tablespoon **extra virgin
olive oil,** plus extra to drizzle

Make the pizza dough. Sift the flour into a bowl and stir in the salt and yeast. Make a well in the middle and gradually work in the measured water and the oil until the mixture comes together in a ball. Transfer to a lightly floured surface and knead for 8–10 minutes or until the dough is smooth. Place in an oiled bowl, cover with clingfilm and leave to rise for 1 hour until doubled in size.

Knock the air from the dough and cut in half. Roll one piece out on a floured surface to form a 23 cm (9 inch) round. Lightly spray a heavy-based frying pan with oil and press the dough into the base. Spread half the pesto over the dough and top with half the tomatoes, mozzarella and olives, some salt and pepper and a drizzle more oil.

Place the pan on a moderately hot barbecue, cover with the barbecue lid or a wok lid and cook for 10–12 minutes until the dough is crisp underneath and the cheese melted. Carefully slide the pizza out on to a board, garnish with half the basil leaves and serve hot. Make the second pizza.

For garlic & rosemary pizza, follow the recipe above to make the pizza dough and roll out to the required size. Combine 2 crushed garlic cloves, 1 tablespoon chopped rosemary, some salt and pepper and 4 tablespoons extra virgin olive oil. Cook the pizza bases following the method above, but this time turn halfway through with a palette knife, so that both sides brown. Remove from the heat and brush each one with the garlic and rosemary oil. Serve hot.

144

sesame-lime buttered sweetcorn

Serves **6**
Preparation time **15 minutes**,
  plus chilling
Cooking time **25–30 minutes**

1 tablespoon **sesame seeds**
4 tablespoons **unsalted
  butter**, softened
1 small **red chilli**, deseeded
  and finely chopped
grated rind and juice of ½–1
  lime, plus extra rind to
  garnish
3 small **sweetcorn cobs**
salt and **black pepper**
watercress, to garnish

Dry-fry the sesame seeds in a small frying pan until golden. Leave to cool slightly, then place in a food processor or blender with the butter, chilli, lime rind and juice and salt and pepper to taste and blend until combined. Transfer the butter to a piece of foil and roll into a sausage shape. Chill for 30 minutes, then remove from the foil and cut into thin slices.

Parboil the sweetcorn cobs for 5 minutes, then cut into 1 cm (½ inch) slices. Place on double-thickness pieces of foil, top with the butter slices and wrap up the foil parcels tightly. Cook on a hot barbecue for 20–25 minutes until the corn is tender. Garnish with lime rind and some watercress and serve immediately with more butter slices.

For coriander & chilli butter, instead of the sesame-lime butter, combine 125 g (4 oz) softened butter with 2 tablespoons chopped fresh coriander, 1 deseeded and finely chopped red chilli and some black pepper. Mash well and wrap and chill as above. Serve in slices with barbecued foods.

potato skins & soured cream dip

Serves **6**
Preparation time **8 minutes**
Cooking time **4 minutes**

6 large **potatoes**, baked and
  left to go cold
150 g (5 oz) grated **Cheddar
  cheese**
spray oil

Dip
200 g (7 oz) **soured cream**
1 **garlic clove**, crushed
1 tablespoon chopped **chives**
salt and **black pepper**

Take the cooled potatoes and cut into quarters. Scoop out and discard the potato flesh (or use for another recipe). Transfer the skins to a bowl and spray with a little oil.

Cook the skins cut-side down on the barbecue for 2 minutes, turn and carefully sprinkle a little cheese on to each skin. Cook for a further 2 minutes until the cheese is melted.

Meanwhile, make the dip. Combine the ingredients in a bowl and season to taste. Serve the skins with the dipping sauce.

For new potato skewers, parboil 20 small new potatoes for 10 minutes, drain and refresh under cold water. Pat dry and thread the potatoes on to 4 pre-soaked bamboo skewers. Spray with a little oil and cook on a hot barbecue for 5–6 minutes on each side until the potatoes are charred and cooked through. Serve with Aïoli (see page 122).

moroccan carrot salad

Serves **4–6**
Preparation time **10 minutes**
Cooking time **15–20 minutes**

2 bunches of **carrots**, trimmed
spray oil
3 tablespoons **sunflower seeds**, toasted
2 tablespoons chopped **parsley**

Dressing
4 tablespoons **extra virgin olive oil**
2 tablespoons **white wine vinegar**
1 **garlic clove**, finely chopped
1 teaspoon **pomegranate syrup**
1 teaspoon **clear honey**
salt and **black pepper**

Blanch the carrots in a large pan of lightly salted boiling water for 10 minutes. Drain well and pat dry. Transfer to a bowl and spray with a little oil, then cook on a hot barbecue for 5–10 minutes, turning frequently, until charred.

Meanwhile, combine the dressing ingredients in a large bowl and season to taste. Stir in the cooked carrots, sunflower seeds and parsley and toss well. Serve hot.

For grilled carrots with mustard & chive butter, follow the above recipe to cook the carrots. Meanwhile, beat 50 g (2 oz) softened butter with 2 teaspoons wholegrain mustard, 1 tablespoon snipped chives and a little pepper. Toss the cooked carrots with the butter until coated and serve hot.

vegetable kebabs with tabbouleh

Serves **4**
Preparation time **15 minutes**,
    plus marinating
Cooking time **10–15 minutes**

1 tablespoon chopped
    rosemary
2 **courgettes**, thickly sliced
1 large **red pepper**, deseeded
    and quartered
16 **button mushrooms**,
    trimmed
16 large **cherry tomatoes**
ready-made or **homemade**
    tzatziki (see below), to serve

Tabbouleh
300 g (10 oz) **bulgar wheat**
4 tablespoons each chopped
    coriander, parsley and **mint**
2 **tomatoes**, diced
150 ml (5 fl oz) **extra virgin**
    olive oil
3 tablespoons **red wine**
    vinegar
salt and **pepper**

Put the bulgar wheat in a bowl, pour enough water over to cover the wheat by 5 cm (2 inches) and leave to soak for 20 minutes. Drain well, then stir in the coriander, mint, parsley, tomatoes, 125 ml (4 fl oz) of the oil, vinegar and salt and pepper.

Meanwhile, in a large bowl combine the rosemary with the remaining oil and some salt and pepper. Add the courgette, pepper, mushrooms and cherry tomatoes to the oil, toss well and marinate for 15 minutes. Thread on to metal skewers.

Cook the kebabs on a hot barbecue for 10–15 minutes, turning halfway through, until all the vegetables are cooked. Serve with the tabbouleh and some tzatziki.

For homemade tzatziki, finely grate 1 cucumber and squeeze out as much water as possible. Stir into 200 g (7 oz) Greek-style yogurt with 1 crushed garlic clove, 1 tablespoon chopped mint and a little salt and pepper.

mushroom burgers with onion jam

Serves **4**
Preparation time **5 minutes**,
  plus cooling
Cooking time **30—40 minutes**

8 large **flat mushrooms**,
  trimmed
1 tablespoon **extra virgin
  olive oil**
4 **ciabatta rolls**
50 g (2 oz) **baby spinach
  leaves**
salt and **black pepper**
Aïoli (see page 122), to serve
  (optional)

Onion jam
4 tablespoons **extra virgin
  olive oil**
4 **onions**, thinly sliced
4 **thyme sprigs**, lightly
  bruised
100 g (3½ oz) **light brown
  soft sugar**
100 ml (3½ fl oz) **red wine
  vinegar**
4 tablespoons **redcurrant jelly**

Make the onion jam. Heat the oil in a saucepan and gently fry the onions, thyme sprigs and some salt and pepper for 20—25 minutes until really soft and golden. Discard the thyme sprigs and stir in the sugar, vinegar and redcurrant jelly. Simmer for 6—8 minutes until the sauce is thick and jam-like, then leave to cool completely.

Brush the mushrooms with the oil and season with salt and pepper. Cook on a hot barbecue for 2—3 minutes on each side. Meanwhile, toast the ciabatta rolls for about 1 minute on each side until lightly browned.

Fill each roll with two mushrooms and some spinach leaves and spoon in some onion jam and aïoli, if liked. Serve at once.

For garlic mushroom parcels, trim 500 g (1 lb) button mushrooms and divide between 4 large sheets of foil. Top each pile of mushrooms with 25 g (1 oz) butter, a little crushed garlic, a thyme sprig and some salt and black pepper. Wrap the foil around the mushrooms to seal well and cook on a hot barbecue for 10—12 minutes. Carefully open the parcels and garnish with a little chopped parsley and a squeeze of lemon juice.

chilli squash with couscous salad

Serves **4–6**
Preparation time **15 minutes**
Cooking time **20 minutes**

1 small **butternut squash**,
   about 1 kg (2 lb)
2 tablespoons **extra virgin
   olive oil**
1 tablespoon **balsamic
   vinegar**
1 teaspoon **hot chilli sauce**
1 teaspoon **clear honey**
salt and **black pepper**

Couscous salad
250 g (8 oz) **couscous**
250 ml (8 fl oz) hot **vegetable
   stock**
4 **spring onions**, finely
   chopped
2 tablespoons chopped
   preserved lemon
50 g (2 oz) **raisins**
50 g (2 oz) **pine nuts**, toasted
4 tablespoons chopped
   herbs, such as **coriander**,
   mint and **parsley**
juice of ½ **lemon**

Cut the squash in half and scoop out and discard the seeds, then crossways into 1 cm (½ inch) thick slices. Place in a large bowl with half the oil and some salt and pepper and stir well to coat the squash. Cook on a medium barbecue for about 10 minutes on each side until charred and tender. Return to the bowl and add the remaining oil, balsamic vinegar, chilli sauce and honey and stir well.

Meanwhile, make the salad. Place the couscous in a bowl and pour over the stock. Leave to soak for 10 minutes, then fluff up the grains with a fork. Stir in the remaining ingredients and season to taste. Serve the couscous salad with the squash.

For grilled squash, onion & feta salad, follow the method above to cook the squash. Cut 1 red onion into thick wedges, brush with a little olive oil and barbecue for 3–4 minutes on each side until charred and tender. Place the squash and onion in a bowl, add 125 g (4 oz) rocket leaves, 125 g (4 oz) diced feta cheese, 25 g (1 oz) toasted walnut pieces, 2 tablespoons walnut oil, 2 teaspoons sherry vinegar and some salt and pepper, toss well and serve.

mediterranean burgers with pesto

Serves **4**
Preparation time **15 minutes**
Cooking time **4–6 minutes**

1 **aubergine**, cut into long
strips about 2 mm (⅛ inch)
thick
2 **courgettes**, cut into long
strips about 2 mm (⅛ inch)
thick
3 tablespoons **extra virgin
olive oil**
4 **ciabatta rolls**, halved
2 **tomatoes**, sliced
150 g (5 oz) **buffalo
mozzarella cheese**, sliced
125 g (4 oz) **rocket leaves**

Pesto
50 g (2 oz) **basil**
1 **garlic clove**, crushed
2 tablespoons **pine nuts**,
toasted
¼ teaspoon **sea salt**
6–8 tablespoons **extra virgin
olive oil**
2 tablespoons freshly grated
Parmesan cheese
black pepper

Make the pesto. Place the basil, garlic, pine nuts and
sea salt in a mortar and grind with a pestle to form a
fairly smooth paste. Slowly add the oil until you reach
the required texture (soft but not runny), then finally
add the cheese and pepper, to taste.

Brush the aubergine and courgettes strips with the
oil and season with salt and pepper. Cook on a hot
barbecue for 2–3 minutes on each side until charred
and tender.

Spread the rolls with some pesto, then fill with the
grilled vegetables, tomatoes, mozzarella and rocket.
Add a little extra pesto and serve hot.

For mayonnaise, instead of the pesto, place 3 egg
yolks, 2 teaspoons white wine vinegar, 1 teaspoon
Dijon mustard and a little salt and pepper in a bowl
and, using an electric whisk, beat until the mixture is
frothy. Then very gradually whisk in 300 ml (½ pint)
olive oil, a little at a time, whisking well after each
addition until the sauce is thickened and glossy and
all the oil incorporated. Thin the sauce with a little
boiling water, if too thick. Use as required or cover the
surface with clingfilm and refrigerate for up to 3 days.

salads, sauces & marinades

mixed leaf & courgette salad

Serves **4**
Preparation time **10 minutes**
Cooking time **10 minutes**

4 **courgettes**, cut into thick
  slices
olive oil, for brushing
125 g (4 oz) **mixed salad
  leaves**
handful of **mint leaves**, torn

Dressing
25 g (1 oz) **pine nuts**
4 tablespoons **extra virgin
  olive oil**
2 teaspoons **lemon juice**
1 teaspoon **clear honey**
salt and **black pepper**

Brush the courgette slices with a little oil, then season. Cook on a hot barbecue for 2–3 minutes on each side, then set aside to cool. When cool, place in a bowl with the salad leaves and mint and stir well.

Make the dressing. Place the nuts in a frying pan and heat until golden, shaking the pan so they cook evenly. Transfer to a mortar and bash lightly with a pestle until 'smashed'. Transfer to a bowl and whisk in the oil, lemon juice, honey and some salt and pepper to taste. Add to the salad and toss before serving.

For mixed leaf salad with bacon & croutons, dice 250 g (8 oz) smoked bacon. Heat a frying pan until hot, add the bacon and stir-fry for 3–4 minutes until crisp and the fat is released. Remove the bacon with a slotted spoon and set aside. Add 2 tablespoons extra virgin olive oil to the pan and gently fry 125 g (4 oz) cubed bread for 4–5 minutes until crisp. Drain on kitchen paper. Place the bacon, bread and 125 g (4 oz) mixed salad leaves in a bowl, drizzle over a little more oil, 1–2 teaspoons white wine vinegar and some salt and black pepper. Toss well and serve.

162

pear & pecorino salad

Serves **4**
Preparation time **10 minutes**
Cooking time **2–4 minutes**

4 **pears**, peeled
250 g (8 oz) **rocket**
4 tablespoons **olive oil**
2 tablespoons **balsamic vinegar**
150 g (5 oz) **pecorino cheese**
salt and **black pepper**

Quarter and core the pears, then slice each quarter in half. Thread on to metal skewers, then place on a hot barbecue and cook for 1–2 minutes on each side.

Place the rocket in a bowl with the olive oil, balsamic vinegar and a little salt and pepper and toss well.

Peel the pecorino into long ribbons using a vegetable peeler and add to the rocket. Arrange the mixture on 4 individual plates and place the barbecued pears on top. Serve immediately.

For bruschetta with pear & pecorino salad, brush 4 thick slices of sourdough bread with extra virgin olive oil. Toast on a hot barbecue for 1 minute on each side, then rub all over with a peeled garlic clove. Make the salad as above and spoon on to the bruschetta, drizzling a little more oil over the top.

tuna tataki salad & asian dressing

Serves **4**
Preparation time **10 minutes**
Cooking time **3 minutes**

4 **tuna loin fillets** or **steak**,
about 200 g (7 oz) each
(note that the tuna must be
very fresh as it is partly raw
when eaten)
2 teaspoons **sesame oil**
250 g (8 oz) thin **asparagus**,
trimmed
100 g (3½ oz) **mixed salad
leaves**
salt and **black pepper**

**Sesame, soy & ginger
dressing**
1 tablespoon **sunflower oil**
1 tablespoon **cold water**
4 teaspoons **rice wine
vinegar**
1 tablespoon **soy sauce**
1½ teaspoons **caster sugar**
1 teaspoon peeled and grated
fresh root ginger
1 teaspoon **sesame oil**

Brush the tuna with sesame oil and season well
with salt and pepper. Cook on a hot barbecue for
10 seconds on each side, then rinse under cold water
to stop the fish cooking further. Pat dry and set aside.

Stir the dressing ingredients together in a bowl and
season to taste.

Blanch the asparagus in lightly salted boiling water
for 2 minutes. Drain well, refresh under cold water
and pat dry.

Arrange the salad leaves and asparagus on a large
platter. Slice the tuna thinly and arrange with the
salad. Drizzle with the dressing and serve.

For seared tuna with chilli jam, lightly season
4 x 200 g (7 oz) tuna steaks, brush with oil and cook
on a hot barbecue for 1 minute on each side. Rest
briefly, then serve with Chilli Jam (see page 114).

mushroom & watercress salad

Serves **4**
Preparation time **10 minutes**
Cooking time **22 minutes**

4 slices of **rustic bread**
4 large **flat mushrooms**,
   trimmed
125 g (4 oz) **soft goats'
   cheese**
3 tablespoons **olive oil**
1 tablespoon **cider vinegar**
125 g (4 oz) **watercress**
sea salt and **mixed
   peppercorns**, crushed

Toast the bread slices on a medium barbecue for 1 minute on each side until browned. Set aside, keeping warm.

Place the mushrooms on the barbecue, gills down, and cook for 10 minutes. Turn the mushrooms over and cook for another 10 minutes. (The undersides are cooked first to seal in all the juices.)

Place the toasted bread on 4 plates and spread each slice with some goats' cheese. Mix together the olive oil, vinegar and seasoning in a small jug to make a dressing.

Remove the cooked mushrooms from the barbecue and slice. Mix them with the watercress and dressing and heap on to the toasted bread. Serve immediately.

For grilled mushrooms with lemon & thyme butter, beat 2 tablespoons chopped fresh thyme and the grated rind of 1 lemon into 125 g (4 oz) butter with a little pepper. Trim 8 large flat mushrooms, spray with olive oil and cook, stem side up, on a medium-hot barbecue for 2–3 minutes. Turn over and dot with the butter, then grill for a further 3–4 minutes until the mushrooms are tender. Serve with 4 slices of toasted bread.

root vegetable & rocket salad

Serves **4**
Preparation time **15 minutes**
Cooking time **40—55 minutes**

1 bunch of small **beetroot**, trimmed
1 bunch of **carrots**, trimmed
1 **red onion**, cut into thick wedges
spray oil
125 g (4 oz) **baby rocket**
100 g (3½ oz) **pecan nuts**, toasted

Dressing
100 g (3½ oz) **soft goats' cheese**
4 teaspoons **white wine vinegar**
2 teaspoons **clear honey**
125 ml (4 fl oz) **extra virgin olive oil**, plus extra for brushing
2—3 tablespoons boiling **water**
salt and **black pepper**

Place the beetroot in a pan of cold water, bring to the boil and simmer for 20—30 minutes, then remove with a slotted spoon. Add the carrots to the pan and cook for 5 minutes. Cut the beetroot into wedges and thread on to 2 metal skewers.

Spray the beetroots and carrots with a little oil and cook on a hot barbecue for 8—10 minutes on each side. Meanwhile, thread the onion wedges on to 2 metal skewers, spray with oil and barbecue for 5 minutes on each side.

Place the beetroot, carrots and onion in a bowl with the rocket and pecan nuts.

Make the dressing. Blend the ingredients together in a food processor or blender until smooth and season to taste. Arrange the salad on a platter and serve drizzled with the goats' cheese dressing.

For tangy mustard vinaigrette, instead of the dressing, whisk together 3 tablespoons extra virgin olive oil, 1 tablespoon red wine vinegar, 2 teaspoons whole grain mustard, a pinch of caster sugar and some salt and black pepper. Prepare the salad as above, and serve with the mustard vinaigrette drizzled over.

chickpea & vegetable salad

Serves **4**
Preparation time **10 minutes**
Cooking time **8 minutes**

4 shallots
2 **garlic cloves**, sliced
4 large **red Spanish chillies**,
   halved lengthways and
   deseeded
300 g (10 oz) can **chickpeas**,
   rinsed and drained
1 bunch of **mint**, roughly
   chopped
3 tablespoons **olive oil**
4 tablespoons **lemon juice**
salt and **black pepper**

Heat a ridged grill pan. Cut the shallots into wedges, keeping the root ends intact to hold the wedges together, and thread them on to a metal skewer. Thread the garlic cloves on to another skewer and the chillies on to a third.

Place all the skewers on a hot barbecue and cook the garlic for 1 minute on each side, the chillies for 2–3 minutes on each side and the shallots for 4 minutes on each side. Remove and place the vegetables in a large bowl.

Add the drained chickpeas, chopped mint, olive oil, lemon juice and seasoning to the bowl of griddled vegetables. Mix all the ingredients together roughly and serve.

For bulgar wheat & grilled vegetable salad, cook the vegetables as above and make a double quantity of the dressing (without the chickpeas). Meanwhile, soak 150 g (5 oz) dried bulgar wheat in about 600 ml (1 pint) boiling water for 20 minutes, then drain and toss with the vegetables and dressing.

smoked garlic caesar salad

Serves **4**
Preparation time **10 minutes**
Cooking time **10–12 minutes**

2 large slices of **sourdough bread**
olive oil, for brushing
4 **streaky bacon rashers**
2 **cos lettuce hearts**, torn
12 drained **anchovy fillets**
2 **eggs**, hard-boiled, shelled and quartered

Dressing
3 **garlic cloves**
1 **egg yolk**
2 teaspoons **white wine vinegar**
4 drained **anchovy fillets**
75 ml (3 fl oz) **olive oil**
3 tablespoons freshly grated **Parmesan cheese**
salt and **black pepper**

Start by making the dressing. Thread the garlic cloves on to a metal skewer and cook on a medium barbecue for 6–8 minutes until soft and lightly charred. Leave to cool. Place the garlic in a food processor or blender with the remaining ingredients and blend until smooth. Add a little boiling water to thin the sauce, if necessary.

Brush the sourdough bread with a little oil and toast for 1 minute on each side until browned. Cut into cubes and place in a large bowl. Barbecue the bacon until crisp, then leave to cool and tear into bite-sized pieces. Add the lettuce leaves, anchovies and egg quarters. Drizzle the dressing over the salad, toss well and serve.

For grilled chicken Caesar salad, cut 2 x 250 g (8 oz) chicken breast fillets in half horizontally so you have 4 thin steaks. Season well, brush with oil and barbecue on a high heat for 4–5 minutes on each side. Cut into strips and toss with the salad above.

pepper & asparagus salad

Serves **4**
Preparation time **10 minutes**
Cooking time **10 minutes**

4 **red peppers**, quartered,
  cored and deseeded
200 g (7 oz) **asparagus**,
  trimmed
2 **red chillies**
4 tablespoons **olive oil**
1 tablespoon **balsamic
  vinegar**
75 g (3 oz) **Parmesan
  cheese**
salt and **black pepper**

Cook the pepper quarters and asparagus on a hot barbecue for 5 minutes on each side, then set aside. Meanwhile, cook the chillies, turning frequently, for a total of 3 minutes, then set aside.

Deseed the red chillies and cut the flesh into very thin strips.

Arrange the vegetables on a serving plate. Drizzle with the oil and balsamic vinegar and sprinkle with salt and pepper. Peel thin ribbons of Parmesan, using a vegetable peeler, and scatter over the vegetables. Serve with bread toasted on the barbecue or as a side dish to accompany barbecued fish or poultry.

For pepper, asparagus & goats' cheese tortilla wraps, cook the peppers, asparagus and chillies as above and slice the chillies. Divide the cooked vegetables between 4 flour tortillas and top each with 25 g (1 oz) crumbled goats' cheese and a handful of rocket leaves. Roll the tortillas up and serve.

beef salad with mustard dressing

Serves **4**
Preparation time **15 minutes**
Cooking time **8–10 minutes**

4 **beef fillet steaks**, about
200 g (7 oz) each
olive oil, for brushing and
drizzling
2 tablespoons chopped
thyme
4 slices of **sourdough bread**
2 **garlic cloves**
50 g (2 oz) **watercress
leaves**
50 g (2 oz) **wild rocket
leaves**
2 tablespoons drained **capers**
salt and **black pepper**

Dressing
3 tablespoons **crème fraîche**
1 tablespoon **wholegrain
mustard**
1 teaspoon **white wine
vinegar**
2 tablespoons snipped **chives**
1 tablespoon boiling **water**

Brush the beef with oil and rub in the thyme, salt and
pepper. Cook on a medium barbecue for 3–4 minutes
on each side. Rest in foil for 5 minutes, then slice thinly.

Meanwhile, to make the dressing, whisk the crème
fraîche, mustard, vinegar and chives together, then
gradually whisk in the measured water and some
salt and pepper until evenly blended.

Toast the bread slices on the barbecue for 1 minute
on each side until browned. Rub with the garlic and
drizzle with oil. Top each with some salad leaves,
capers and beef slices and pour the dressing over.

For chargrilled beef fillet with walnut pesto, place
50 g (2 oz) walnuts, 25 g (1 oz) drained cornichons,
1 crushed garlic clove,1 tablespoon drained capers,
2 tablespoons chopped parsley, 6 tablespoons extra
virgin olive oil and some salt and pepper in a food
processor or blender and blend until fairly smooth.
Cook the beef steaks following the above method and
serve topped with the pesto and a Tomato & Olive
Salad (see page 86).

mediterranean couscous salad

Serves **4**
Preparation time **15 minutes**
Cooking time **10 minutes**

2 **red onions**
2 **garlic cloves**
2 **green chillies**
1 **aubergine**, sliced
1 **red pepper**
1 **courgette**, sliced
  lengthways
125 g (4 oz) **couscous**
½ teaspoon **cumin**
½ teaspoon **paprika**
pinch of **dried chilli flakes**
5 tablespoons **olive oil**
salt and **black pepper**

To garnish
1 bunch of **coriander**,
  chopped
1 **lemon**, griddled and cut into
  wedges (optional)

Cut the red onions into wedges, keeping the root ends intact to hold the wedges together.

Thread the garlic cloves and chillies on to separate metal skewers, then cook all the vegetables on a hot barbecue as follows, removing them when charred on all sides to a large serving bowl: aubergine, pepper and red onions for 5 minutes on each side; courgette for 4 minutes on each side; chillies for 2–3 minutes on each side and garlic for 1 minute on each side.

Place the couscous in a bowl and add enough hot water to cover. Leave for 5 minutes to allow all the water to be absorbed.

Peel the chillies and pepper when cool enough to handle, then deseed them. Roughly chop all the vegetables and add them to the bowl of couscous. Add the cumin, paprika, chilli flakes and seasoning, and mix well. Drizzle with the olive oil and garnish with the chopped coriander and lemon wedges, if using.

For grilled vegetable, feta & mint salad, prepare and cook all the vegetables as above and combine in a large bowl. Add 200 g (7 oz) crumbled feta cheese, 125 g (4 oz) pitted black olives and a handful of torn fresh mint leaves. Whisk together 3 tablespoons extra virgin olive oil, the juice of ½ lemon, 1 teaspoon honey, ½ teaspoon ground cumin and some salt and pepper, add to the salad and stir.

parma ham & vegetable salad

Serves **4**
Preparation time **10 minutes**
Cooking time **18 minutes**

2 **red onions**
2 **red peppers**, cored, deseeded and cut into large pieces
2 **courgettes**, cut into long lengths
1 **aubergine**, cut into long lengths
1 bunch of **asparagus**, trimmed
8 slices of **Parma ham**
1 bunch of **basil**, roughly chopped
4 tablespoons **olive oil**
2 tablespoons **balsamic vinegar**
salt and **black pepper**
basil sprig, to garnish

Cut the red onions into wedges, keeping the root ends intact to hold the wedges together. Cook all the vegetables on a hot barbecue as follows, removing them when cooked to a large serving bowl: onions for 5 minutes on each side; red peppers for 5 minutes on the skin side only; courgettes for 3 minutes on each side; aubergine for 4 minutes on each side, and the asparagus for 4 minutes on one side only. (If all the vegetables are put on at the same time, you will need to remove them in the following order: asparagus, peppers, courgettes, aubergine, onions.) When all the vegetables have been barbecued, toss them together well in the bowl.

Place the slices of Parma ham on the grill rack to cook for 4 minutes on each side, or until crispy.

Add the basil to the vegetables with the olive oil, balsamic vinegar and a little seasoning. Top the vegetables with the crispy Parma ham and serve immediately, garnished with a sprig of basil.

For beef fillet & vegetable salad, season a 750 g (1½ lb) beef fillet and brush with oil. Cook on a medium-hot barbecue for 25 minutes, turning halfway through, then wrap in foil and leave to rest for 10 minutes. Meanwhile, prepare and cook the vegetables as above and add the dressing, omitting the Parma ham. Slice the beef fillet thickly and serve with the grilled vegetable salad.

cypriot chicken & haloumi salad

Serves **4**
Preparation time **20 minutes**,
  plus marinating
Cooking time **20–24 minutes**

3 skinless **chicken breast
  fillets**, about 125 g (4 oz)
  each
1 bunch of **oregano**, chopped
1 tablespoon **olive oil**
250 g (8 oz) **haloumi cheese**
salt and **black pepper**

Cypriot salad
1 **cucumber**, skinned,
  deseeded and cut
  lengthways into short batons
4 **beefsteak tomatoes**,
  skinned, deseeded and cut
  into wedges
1 **red onion**, finely chopped
1 bunch of **flat leaf parsley**,
  roughly chopped
3 tablespoons **olive oil**
1 tablespoon **wine vinegar**
salt and **black pepper**

Place the chicken in a bowl. Add the chopped oregano, olive oil and seasoning. Leave to marinate at room temperature for 2 hours.

Cook the chicken on a hot barbecue for about 6–8 minutes on each side, then remove, cut into chunks and keep warm.

Meanwhile, make the salad. Place the cucumber, tomato wedges, chopped red onion and parsley in a bowl. Add the olive oil and wine vinegar, toss well and season to taste.

Slice the haloumi into 8 and griddle the slices for 4 minutes on each side then serve with the chicken and salad.

For grilled haloumi with lemon, cut 250 g (8 oz) haloumi cheese into 12 slices and cook on a preheated flat plate (gas barbecue) or in a ridged griddle pan (charcoal barbecue) for 1 minute on each side until charred. Transfer to a platter and immediately squeeze over the juice of ½ lemon, drizzle with a little oil and dress with some chopped fresh parsley. Serve at once.

lime yogurt marinade

Makes **250 ml (8 fl oz)**
Preparation time **5 minutes**,
  plus chilling

150 g (5 oz) **natural yogurt**
2 tablespoons chopped **mint**
grated rind and juice of ½ **lime**
1 **garlic clove**, crushed
½ teaspoon **cumin**
pinch of **caster sugar**
salt and **black pepper**

Place all the ingredients in a bowl and season to taste. Cover the bowl and chill for 1 hour for the flavours to infuse. Use as required.

For tandoori marinade, combine 150 g (5 oz) natural yogurt with 2 crushed garlic cloves, 2 teaspoons peeled and grated fresh root ginger, 2 teaspoons ready-made tandoori spice paste, 2 teaspoons lemon juice and a little salt and pepper. Use to marinate chicken thigh fillets and cook on a hot barbecue.

barbecue sauce with chocolate

Makes **200 ml (7 fl oz)**
Preparation time **5 minutes**
Cooking time **20 minutes**

2 tablespoons **olive oil**
1 small **onion**, finely chopped
1 **garlic clove**, crushed
2 teaspoons **ground
coriander**
1 teaspoon **ground cumin**
½ teaspoon **ground cinnamon**
400 g (13 oz) can **chopped
tomatoes**
3 tablespoons **maple syrup**
3 tablespoons **red wine
vinegar**
1–2 teaspoons **hot chilli
sauce**
15 g (½ oz) **dark chocolate**,
chopped
salt and **pepper**

Heat the oil in a saucepan and gently fry the onion, garlic and spices for 10 minutes until soft but not browned. Add the tomatoes, maple syrup, vinegar, chilli sauce and some salt and pepper and bring to the boil. Simmer gently for 10 minutes, stir in the chocolate until melted and leave to cool.

Transfer to a food processor or blender and blend until smooth. Use as required or store in an airtight container in the refrigerator for up to 1 week.

For sweet chilli barbecue sauce, combine 2 tablespoons tomato paste with 2 tablespoons sweet chilli sauce and 1 tablespoon dark soy sauce, season with a little pepper. Use to baste chicken before cooking on a hot barbecue.

moroccan spice paste

Makes **150 ml (¼ pint)**
Preparation time **5 minutes**

1 bunch of **coriander**,
  including roots, roughly
  chopped
1 bunch of **parsley**, roughly
  chopped
125 ml (4 fl oz) **extra virgin
  olive oil**
2 **garlic cloves**, roughly
  chopped
2 teaspoons **white wine
  vinegar**
1 teaspoon **lemon juice**
1 teaspoon **ground coriander**
1 teaspoon **paprika**
1 teaspoon **ground cumin**
salt and **cayenne pepper**,
  to taste

Place the coriander and parsley, including the stems
and roots, in a food processor or blender. Add all of
the remaining ingredients and blend to form a
smooth paste.

Use as required or store in an airtight container in
the refrigerator for up to 3 days.

For spicy herb paste, blend together 4 tablespoons
chopped herbs such as parsley, basil, mint and
coriander, 2 chopped garlic cloves, 1 deseeded and
chopped large green chilli, grated rind of 1 lemon,
125 ml (4 fl oz) extra virgin olive oil and some salt
and pepper. Use to marinate chicken or fish fillets.

rosemary, coriander & lemon rub

Makes **5 tablespoons**
Cooking time **2–3 minutes**
Preparation time **5 minutes**

2 tablespoons **coriander seeds**
2 tablespoons chopped **rosemary**
grated rind of 1 **lemon**
salt and **black pepper**

Dry-fry the coriander seeds in a frying pan over a high heat for 2–3 minutes until they begin to pop and release their aroma. Cool the spices and mix with the rosemary, lemon rind and some salt and pepper.

Use as required or store in an airtight container for up to 2 weeks.

For fennel rub, dry-fry 2 tablespoons fennel seeds and 1 tablespoon black peppercorns in a small frying pan over a medium heat for 1–2 minutes until they begin to brown and release their aroma. Leave to cool then grind in a spice grinder until fairly fine. Transfer to a bowl and stir in ¼ teaspoon salt. Use as required.

smoky barbecue rub

Makes **5 tablespoons**
Preparation time **5 minutes**

1 tablespoon **salt**
1 tablespoon **smoked paprika**
1 teaspoon **ground coriander**
2 teaspoons crushed **black pepper**
2 teaspoons **mustard powder**
1 teaspoon **caster sugar**
¼ teaspoon **cayenne pepper**

Combine the ingredients in a bowl and stir well. Transfer to an airtight container or use as required. This will keep fresh for up to 2 weeks.

For Asian-style barbecue rub, grind together 4 whole star anise, 2 teaspoons Szechuan peppercorns, 1 teaspoon fennel seeds, 1 cinnamon stick and 6 whole cloves. Mix with 2 crushed garlic cloves, the grated rind of 2 limes and 1 teaspoon salt. Store as above or use as required.

smoked garlic oil

Makes **125 ml (4 fl oz)**
Preparation time **10 minutes**,
  plus soaking
Cooking time **30 minutes**

1 **garlic bulb**, unpeeled
250 g (8 oz) **hickory chips**
125 ml (4 fl oz) **extra virgin
  olive oil**
salt and **black pepper**

Place the garlic bulb in a bowl with the wood chips and cover well with cold water. Leave to soak for 30 minutes, then drain.

Lay a double layer of foil about 30 cm (12 inches) square on the work surface and place the wood chips in the centre in a shallow pile. Fold the foil over the chips and seal the edges to form a pillow-shaped parcel. Using a knife, stab a dozen small holes in the top.

Heat the barbecue to medium and, using the indirect cooking method (see page 12), place the foil parcel over the unlit gas burner (or in the centre of the coal barbecue) and place the garlic on the rack in the roasting tin. Cover and cook for 30 minutes.

Remove the garlic, wrap loosely in foil and leave to cool completely. Trim the top of the garlic and squeeze the paste into a pestle and mortar and pound to a paste. Transfer to a jar and add the oil and some salt and pepper. Use as required or store in an airtight container in the refrigerator for up to 3 days.

For rosemary oil, place 2 rosemary sprigs in a clean, dry bottle and top up with extra virgin olive oil, making sure the tops of the rosemary sprigs are covered. Place in a cool dark place for 3–4 days, then drain the oil into a clean jar. Use as required.

citrus, chilli & fresh thyme oil

Makes **600 ml (1 pint)**
Preparation time **5 minutes**,
   plus infusing

rind of **1 lemon**, cut into long,
   thin strips
rind of **1 lime**, cut into long,
   thin strips
1 large **red chilli**, deseeded
   and sliced
6 **thyme sprigs**, bruised
1 teaspoon **black
   peppercorns**, lightly crushed
600 ml (1 pint) **extra virgin
   olive oil**
salt

Place the lemon and lime rinds in a bowl and add the chilli, thyme sprigs, peppercorns and a little salt. Pour in the oil, cover and leave to infuse in a cool, dark place for 3–4 days.

Strain the oil through a fine sieve into a bottle and use as required.

For piri-piri, a fiery chilli oil, pour 600 ml (1 pint) extra virgin olive oil into a bottle and add 2 tablespoons dried red chilli flakes and a pinch of salt. Leave to infuse for 3 days, then use as required, leaving the chilli flakes in the oil.

sweet treats

mango with strawberry ice

Serves **6**
Preparation time **10 minutes**,
  plus freezing
Cooking time **6 minutes**

125 g (4 oz) **granulated
  sugar**
300 ml (½ pint) **water**
grated rind and juice of
  1 lemon
75 ml (3 fl oz) **white rum**
500 g (1 lb) **strawberries**,
  hulled
3 large ripe **mangoes**
2 tablespoons **light brown
  soft sugar**
½ teaspoon **Chinese
  five-spice powder**

Put the granulated sugar, water, lemon rind and juice into a saucepan and heat gently until the sugar is dissolved, then boil for 3 minutes. Remove from the heat and stir in the rum, then leave to cool.

Place the strawberries in a food processor or blender with the cooled syrup and blend until completely smooth. Transfer to a plastic container and freeze. Beat the mixture after 1 hour, then beat again every 30 minutes until you have a soft sorbet texture. Alternatively, churn in an ice cream maker until slushy. Freeze until required.

Cut the mangoes down each side of the stone and then cut each piece in half. Combine the brown sugar and spice powder and dust lightly over the mango portions. Cook on a medium barbecue for 2—3 minutes on each side until charred. Serve with the strawberry ice.

For quick butterscotch sauce, which you could serve with the barbecued mango, mix 200 g (7 oz) Greek yogurt with 4 tablespoons light brown soft sugar and ½ teaspoon vanilla essence.

honeyed strawberry mousses

Serves **6**
Preparation time **30 minutes**,
  plus freezing
Cooking time **2 minutes**

3 tablespoons **water**
3 teaspoons **powdered
  gelatine** or 1 sachet
400 g (13 oz) **strawberries**,
  hulled, plus extra, halved, to
  decorate (optional)
6 teaspoons **set honey**
300 g (10 oz) **fat-free
  fromage frais**
2 **passion fruit**, halved

Put the water in a small cup and sprinkle over the gelatine, making sure that all the powder absorbs water. Set aside for 5 minutes to soak.

Purée half the strawberries with 2 teaspoons of the honey in a food processor or blender until smooth, then pour into a jug.

Stand the cup of gelatine in a small saucepan of simmering water and heat until it dissolves and the liquid is clear.

Stir 3 teaspoons of gelatine into the strawberry purée and divide between 6 individual 150 ml (¼ pint) metal pudding moulds. Freeze for 15 minutes until just set.

Purée the remaining strawberries with the remaining honey. Add the fromage frais and blend together. Gradually mix in the remaining gelatine and pour over the set strawberry layer in the pudding moulds. Freeze for 4–5 hours until set.

Dip each mould into just-boiled water, count to 5, loosen the edges with a fingertip, then invert each one on to a plate. Holding plate and mould together, jerk to release the mousse. Spoon passion fruit seeds around the desserts and decorate with halved strawberries, if liked.

For strawberry skewers with chocolate dipping sauce, make some chocolate sauce (see page 208). Meanwhile, thread 20 large strawberries on to soaked bamboo skewers, sprinkle with a little icing sugar and cook on a hot barbecue for 2 minutes until starting to sizzle and ooze. Serve with the chocolate sauce.

soufflé omelette with strawberries

Serves **4**
Preparation time **15 minutes**
Cooking time **8–10 minutes**

375 g (12 oz) **strawberries**,
  hulled and thickly sliced, plus
  extra to decorate
2 tablespoons **redcurrant jelly**
2 teaspoons **balsamic
  vinegar**
5 **eggs**, separated
4 tablespoons **icing sugar**,
  sifted
25 g (1 oz) **butter**

Warm the sliced strawberries, redcurrant jelly and vinegar together in a saucepan until the jelly has just melted.

Meanwhile, whisk the egg whites into stiff, moist-looking peaks. Mix the egg yolks with 1 tablespoon of the sugar, then fold into the egg whites.

Heat the butter in a large frying pan, add the egg mixture and cook over a medium heat for 3–4 minutes until the underside is golden. Quickly transfer the pan to a hot grill and cook for 2–3 minutes until the top is browned and the centre still slightly soft, making sure that the handle is away from the heat.

Spoon the warm strawberry mixture over the omelette, fold in half and dust with the remaining sugar. Cut into 4 and serve immediately with extra strawberries.

For sweet soufflé omelette with cherries & cinnamon ice cream, make the omelette following the recipe above. Strain 250 g (8 oz) canned or bottled pitted morello cherries and serve with the omelette and a spoonful of cinnamon ice cream.

chocolate & banana melt

Serves **4**
Preparation time **5 minutes**
Cooking time **2–4 minutes**

8 slices of **white bread**, crusts
  removed
75 g (3 oz) **dark chocolate**,
  finely chopped
1 large **banana**, sliced
50 g (2 oz) **marshmallows**,
  chopped
spray oil

Place half the bread slices on the work surface and top each with chocolate, banana and marshmallows. Top with the remaining bread.

Spray the sandwiches with oil and cook on the flat plate of a gas barbecue or on a rack over charcoal for 1–2 minutes. Spray the top side with a little oil, flip and cook for a further 1–2 minutes until golden. Serve with vanilla ice cream, if liked.

For toasted marshmallows with chocolate dipping sauce, combine 175 ml (3 fl oz) single cream, 150 g (5 oz) chopped dark chocolate and 15 g (½ oz) butter in a bowl set over a saucepan of gently simmering water (do not let the bowl touch the water). Stir frequently until the chocolate has melted and the mixture is smooth. Remove from the heat and cool slightly. Spear marshmallows on to metal skewers and cook over a hot barbecue (make sure the marshmallows don't actually touch the grill or you'll have a sticky mess). Serve with the chocolate sauce.

hot barbecued fruit salad

Serves **4**
Preparation time **15 minutes**
Cooking time **8 minutes**

1 small **pineapple**
1 **mango**
1 **nectarine**, quartered and
  pitted
1 **peach**, quartered and pitted
2 **apricots**, halved, or
  quartered if large, and pitted
4 tablespoons **Greek yogurt**
clear honey, for drizzling
few **cardamom seeds**
  (optional)

Top and tail the pineapple and place it on one end on a chopping board. Using a sharp knife, cut downwards to remove the skin, working all around the pineapple. Cut the pineapple flesh into chunks — in a small pineapple the core is usually sweet and soft enough to eat.

Peel the mango and cut it into slices on either side of the stone. Cook the mango and pineapple on a hot barbecue for 4 minutes on each side and the nectarine, peach and apricots for 3 minutes on each side. If you wish, thread the fruit pieces on to metal skewers before cooking.

Arrange the griddled fruit in individual serving dishes. Top each with a tablespoonful of Greek yogurt, drizzle clear honey over the top and scatter with cardamom seeds, if using, or top with spoonfuls of Caramel & Cinnamon Yogurt (see below).

For caramel & cinnamon yogurt, to serve as an accompaniment, combine 200 g (7 oz) Greek yogurt in a bowl with 1 tablespoon dark soft brown sugar and 1 teaspoon ground cinnamon.

lemon & honey ice

Serves **4—6**
Preparation time **20—25 minutes**, plus cooling and freezing
Cooking time **2 minutes**

4 large or 6 medium **lemons**
about 4 tablespoons **water**
2 tablespoons **clear honey**
50 g (2 oz) **caster sugar**
1 **bay leaf** or **lemon balm sprig**
475 ml (16 fl oz) **natural yogurt** or **fromage frais**
strips of **lemon rind**, to decorate

Slice off the top of each lemon. Carefully scoop out all the pulp and juice with a teaspoon. Discard any white pith, skin, and pits, then purée the pulp and juice in a food processor or blender. You will need 150 ml (5 fl oz). If there is less than this, top it up with water.

Put the measured water, honey, sugar and bay leaf into a saucepan. Stir over a low heat until the sugar has dissolved, then leave to cool. Blend the mixture with the lemon purée and the yogurt. Do not remove the herb at this stage.

Pour into a freezer tray or shallow dish and freeze until lightly frozen, then gently fork the mixture and remove the herb. Return the ice to the freezer.

Transfer the ice to the refrigerator about 20 minutes before serving. Serve in individual bowls, decorated with strips of lemon rind.

For strawberry yogurt ice cream, wash and dry 500 g (1 lb) strawberries, place in a blender or food processor with 2 tablespoons honey, 1 teaspoon lemon juice and a few drops of vanilla essence and purée until smooth. Beat in 600 ml (1 pint) Greek yogurt and freeze for 6 hours, beating every hour until frozen.

barbecued bananas & ice cream

Serves **4**

Preparation time **5 minutes,**
  plus infusing and freezing

Cooking time **10 minutes**

4 large **bananas**

Ice cream

500 ml (17 fl oz) **milk**

250 ml (8 fl oz) **double cream**

2 **star anise**, lightly bashed

5 **egg yolks**

125 ml (4 fl oz) **maple syrup**

Start by making the ice cream. Put the milk, cream and star anise into a saucepan and heat until boiling point is reached. Then remove from the heat and infuse for 20 minutes.

Meanwhile, beat the egg yolks and syrup together, then strain in the infused milk and return to the pan. Heat gently, stirring until the custard thickens to coat the back of a wooden spoon. Do not boil. Leave the custard until cold and then freeze in an ice cream maker, according to the manufacturer's instructions.

Place the whole bananas in their skins on the barbecue and cook for 4–5 minutes, turning halfway through until the skins are blackened. Peel and serve the banana with a scoop of ice cream.

For barbecued chocolate bananas, follow the recipe above to cook the bananas, cutting the skins open after 3 minutes. Place 2 squares of dark, milk or white chocolate into the banana flesh and cook for the final 1–2 minutes until the chocolate is melted.

raspberry cheesecake

Serves **6–8**
Preparation time **20 minutes**,
 plus chilling
Cooking time **5 minutes**

50 g (2 oz) **butter**, melted
125 g (4 oz) **digestive
 biscuits**, crushed
3 tablespoons **orange juice**
3 teaspoons **powdered
 gelatine** or 1 sachet
375 g (12 oz) **curd cheese**
50 g (2 oz) **caster sugar**
3 **eggs**, separated
300 ml (½ pint) **double cream**

To decorate
4 tablespoons **double cream**,
 whipped
250 g (8 oz) **raspberries**

Mix the melted butter into the biscuits crumbs and press the mixture into the base of a lightly oiled 20 cm (8 inch) springform cake tin; chill for 20 minutes until firm.

Put the orange juice in a small saucepan, sprinkle over the gelatine and leave to soak for 5 minutes. Heat gently until the gelatine dissolves and the liquid is clear.

Meanwhile, beat the cheese and sugar together in a bowl until smooth then beat in the egg yolks. Stir 2 tablespoons into the gelatine mixture and then stir this back into the main mixture.

Whip the cream until firm and fold into the cheese mixture. In a clean bowl, whisk the egg whites until stiff, stir 2 tablespoons into the cheese mixture to lighten it. Fold in the remaining egg whites until evenly combined.

Spoon the mixture over the biscuit base and level the surface. Chill for 1–1½ hours or until the filling is set. Pipe a whipped cream border around the edge of the cheesecake and arrange the raspberries over the top. Cut into wedges to serve.

For lemon, ginger & blueberry cheesecake, make the biscuit crust using 125 g (4 oz) gingernuts, replace the orange juice with lemon juice and add 2 teaspoons grated lemon rind to the curd cheese, sugar and egg yolks. Serve the cheesecake in wedges with whipped cream and fresh blueberries.

grilled pineapple with granita

Serves **6**
Preparation time **10 minutes**,
  plus freezing
Cooking time **12–14 minutes**

1 **pineapple**, 750 g (1½ lb)
75 g (3 oz) **palm sugar** or
  dark brown soft sugar

Lime & mint granita
250 g (8 oz) **granulated
  sugar**
500 ml (15 fl oz) cold **water**
4 strips of **lime rind**
4 large **mint sprigs**, bruised
250 ml (8 fl oz) **lime juice**
  (from about 6 large limes)
50 ml (2 fl oz) **vodka**

Make the granita. Place the sugar, measured water and lime rind in a saucepan, heat gently to dissolve the sugar and then bring to the boil. Simmer for 5 minutes, remove from the heat and stir in the mint. Leave to cool and then strain.

Stir the lime juice and vodka into the sugar syrup and transfer to a bowl. Place in the freezer for about 4 hours until frozen.

Remove the ice from the freezer for 15 minutes to soften then transfer to a food processor and blend for 30 seconds until soft and pale. Freeze again if necessary.

Top and tail the pineapple and place it on one end on a chopping board. Using a sharp knife, cut downwards to remove the skin, working all around the pineapple. Quarter and core the pineapple, then cut the flesh into wedges. Spike on to 6 metal skewers, dip in the sugar and barbecue over a medium heat for 2–3 minutes on each side until golden. Cool slightly and serve with the granita.

For grilled pineapple lollipops, prepare the pineapple as above but cut the wedges into chunks. Skewer the chunks on to presoaked bamboo skewers, dust with a little palm or brown sugar and cook as above. Serve the lollipops with some Greek yogurt flavoured with clear honey and a squeeze of fresh lemon juice.

strawberry kebabs with ice cream

Serves **4**
Preparation time **5 minutes**
Cooking time **3–4 minutes**

500 g (1 lb) **strawberries**,
 washed but unhulled
500 ml (17 fl oz) carton luxury
 ice cream (such as vanilla,
 strawberry or chocolate)

Soak 8 bamboo skewers in cold water for 30 minutes.
Thread the strawberries on to the skewers and cook
on a hot barbecue for 3–4 minutes, turning frequently.

Meanwhile, spoon scoops of luxury ice cream into
4 serving dishes. Spoon the griddled strawberries
on top and serve.

For grilled figs with ice cream, cut 8 large, just-ripe
figs in half and dust lightly with icing sugar. Cook
on a hot barbecue for 2–3 minutes, tuning halfway
through until tender, then serve with hazelnut or
cinnamon ice cream.

lemon & honeycomb stacks

Serves **2**
Preparation time **6 minutes**
Cooking time **2–4 minutes**

60 ml (2½ fl oz) **double cream**, plus extra to serve
30 g (1½ oz) **honeycomb** or **old-fashioned cinder toffee**, crumbled
1 teaspoon finely grated **lemon rind**
65 g (2½ oz) **candied lemon peel**, finely chopped (optional)
150 ml (5 fl oz) traditional **lemon curd**
6 **Scotch pancakes**
blueberries, to serve

Put the cream, honeycomb, lemon rind, candied peel, if using, and lemon curd in a bowl and mix well. Place a dollop of the lemon cream on a pancake, top with a second pancake and another dollop of lemon cream on top, then finish with a third pancake. Repeat the process so that you have two triple-decker lemon pancakes.

Cook the pancake stacks on a medium-hot barbecue for 1–2 minutes, then flip over and cook for the same time until the outside pancakes are toasted and the lemon cream is beginning to ooze from the sides. Serve immediately with some blueberries.

For sweet bruschetta with lemon cream & honeycomb, make the lemon cream as above. Toast 2 slices of brioche or raisin bread lightly on the barbecue, top with a spoonful of the lemon cream and serve topped with mixed fresh berries dusted with icing sugar.

fruit parcels with caramel sauce

Serves **4**
Preparation time **10 minutes**
Cooking time **15 minutes**

6 figs, quartered
2 peaches, pitted and
quartered
175 g (6 oz) **blueberries**

Caramel sauce
50 g (2 oz) **unsalted butter**
175 g (6 oz) **light brown soft
sugar**
2 tablespoons **golden syrup**
75 ml (3 fl oz) **double cream**
few drops of **vanilla essence**

Make the sauce. Melt the butter in a small saucepan over a medium heat, add the sugar and syrup and cook gently until the sugar dissolves. Stir in the cream and vanilla essence and bring slowly to boiling point. Remove from the heat and leave to stand while cooking the foil parcels.

Lay 4 pieces of foil on the work surface and arrange a pile of the fruit in the middle of each one. Seal the parcels, then cook on a low heat on the barbecue for 8–10 minutes. Carefully open the parcels and serve the fruit topped with the caramel sauce.

For grilled figs with Amaretto cream, cut 6 just-ripe figs in half and sprinkle the cut sides with a little brown sugar. Cook cut-side up on a medium heat for 3–4 minutes until the figs are tender. Meanwhile, lightly whip 150 ml (¼ pint) double cream with 1 tablespoon icing sugar and 1 tablespoon Amaretto liqueur until just firm. Serve with the figs.

fruit salad cups

Serves **6**
Preparation time **45 minutes**
Cooking time **15 minutes**

1 large **mango**
150 g (5 oz) **raspberries**
100 g (3½ oz) **blueberries**
200 g (7 oz) **natural yogurt**
sifted **icing sugar**, to decorate

Tuile cups
2 **egg whites**
50 g (2 oz) **caster sugar**
3 tablespoons **sunflower oil**
few drops of **vanilla extract**
40 g (1½ oz) **plain flour**

Line 3 baking sheets with nonstick baking paper. Put the egg whites in a bowl and fork together until frothy but still clear. Add the sugar, oil and vanilla extract and mix together.

Sift the flour into the bowl and stir together. Spoon the mixture into 6 mounds on the baking sheets and spread each to a circle, about 12 cm (5 inches) across.

Place one of the baking sheets in a preheated oven, 190°C (375°F), Gas Mark 5, for about 5 minutes until the biscuits are light brown in the centre and slightly darker around the edges. Remove from the oven and leave to stand for 30 seconds. Put a second sheet in the oven, then repeat with the third.

Loosen the cooked biscuits. Working quickly, drape each biscuit over a large orange and pinch the edges to make a fluted edge. Leave to set for a few minutes then lift off the oranges, turn up the other way and put on to a wire rack. Repeat to make 6 cups.

Stand the mango on its side and cut a thick slice off each side. Cut the flesh away from the stone and peel and cut the flesh into slices. Mix with the berries. Spoon the yogurt, then the fruit into the cups. Transfer to serving plates, dust with icing sugar and serve immediately with passionfruit sauce (see below).

For passionfruit sauce, heat together in a saucepan 100 g (3 ½ oz) caster sugar and 100 ml (3½ fl oz) water, stirring over a low heat until the sugar dissolves. Add 75 ml (3 oz) passionfruit pulp (from about 6 fruits), bring to the boil and simmer for 10 minutes until it forms a sauce. Leave to cool and serve at room temperature.

raspberry & mascarpone brioche

Serves **4**
Preparation time **5 minutes**
Cooking time **1–2 minutes**

4 slices of **brioche** or **raisin
  bread**
250 g (8 oz) **raspberries**

Vanilla mascarpone
250 g (8 oz) **mascarpone
  cheese**
2 tablespoons **single cream**
seeds from 1 **vanilla pod**
1–2 tablespoons **icing sugar,**
  plus extra to dust

Make the vanilla mascarpone. Stir the mascarpone, cream, vanilla seeds and icing sugar together until smooth – do not overbeat.

Toast the brioche slices on a medium barbecue for 30 seconds on each side until lightly browned. Top with the raspberries and vanilla mascarpone and dust with icing sugar.

For brioche with blistered peaches, cut 6 peaches in half and remove the stones. Dust with a little icing sugar and barbecue on a medium heat for 1–2 minutes on each side until charred and tender. Combine 250 g (8 oz) mascarpone cheese with 2 tablespoons single cream, 1 teaspoon almond essence and a pinch of ground mixed spice. Serve with the peaches.

summer berry roulade

Serves **8**
Preparation time **30 minutes**
Cooking time **20 minutes**

4 eggs
125 g (4 oz) **caster sugar,**
  plus extra for sprinkling
grated rind of 1 **lemon**
125 g (4 oz) **plain flour**

Filling
250 g (8 oz) **fromage frais**
125 g (4 oz) **quark**
1 tablespoon **caster sugar**
125 g (4 oz) **blueberries**
150 g (5 oz) **raspberries**

Line the base and sides of a 30 x 23 cm (12 x 9 inch) Swiss roll tin with a single sheet of nonstick baking paper, cutting the paper in the corners. Put the eggs, sugar and lemon rind in a mixing bowl set over a saucepan of simmering water. With an electric whisk, beat the mixture for 10 minutes until it is thick and the mixture leaves a trail over the surface when the beaters are raised.

Remove the bowl from the saucepan, sift the flour over the surface and gently fold in. Pour the mixture into the tin. Bake in a preheated oven, 200°C (400°F), Gas Mark 6, for 8–10 minutes until the top springs back when pressed with a fingertip.

Put a piece of nonstick baking paper (about the same size as the tin) on the work surface with a narrow edge towards you and sprinkle with sugar. Quickly turn the sponge out on to the paper, peel off the lining paper and cover with a second piece of paper. Loosely roll up the sponge, starting from the edge nearest you. Leave loosely wrapped in the sugared paper to cool.

Unroll the sponge and remove the centre paper. Mix the fromage frais and quark with the sugar and spread over the cake. Sprinkle with the fruit, reserving a few for decoration, then re-roll the sponge, using the sugared paper underneath to help you (but being careful not to roll the paper up inside the roulade) and transfer to a serving plate. Decorate with the remaining fruit and serve cut into thick slices.

bananas, fruit sauce & ice cream

Serves **4**

Preparation time **10 minutes**

Cooking time **25 minutes**

200 g (7 oz) **dried peaches**
or **apricots**

200 ml (7 fl oz) **pineapple
juice**

1 teaspoon **ground cinnamon**

4 **bananas**

vanilla ice cream

Place the peaches or apricots, pineapple juice and cinnamon in a saucepan and bring to the boil. Reduce the heat and simmer for 10 minutes, or until the fruits are soft. Cool slightly, then place in a food processor or blender and process until smooth.

Cook the whole bananas in their skins on a hot barbecue for 4–5 minutes, turning halfway through, until the skins are blackened.

Peel the bananas. Serve each with scoops of vanilla ice cream and spoonfuls of the sauce.

For maple & pecan fudge sauce, an alternative sauce to serve with the grilled bananas, heat 75 g (3 oz) unsalted butter, 75 ml (3 fl oz) maple syrup and 75 ml (3 fl oz) double cream together in a small pan set on a low heat until the butter melts. Simmer for 5 minutes until thickened, then stir in 75 g (3 oz) pecan nuts. Simmer for a further minute, then leave to cool. Serve warm.

index

acknowledgements

Executive Editor: Nicky Hill
Editor: Amy Corbett
Executive Art Editor: Mark Stevens
Designer: Rebecca Johns for Cobalt id
Photographer: Ian Wallace
Food Stylist: Louise Pickford
Production Controller: Carolin Stransky

Commissioned Photography © Octopus Publishing Group Ltd/Ian Wallace apart from the following:
© Octopus Publishing Group Limited/Graham Kirk 35; Gus Filgate 51, 127, 141; Ian Wallace 109, 119, 147, 213; Lis Parsons 207, 223; Peter Myers 95, 101, 131, 217; Sean Myers 103, 165, 169, 173, 177, 181, 183, 185, 211, 221, 233; Stephen Conroy 81, 85; William Lingwood 69, 205, 227, 231; William Reavell 23.